MY FAVOURITE STORIES
OF SCOTLAND

C H Cutt
35 Fonbrught Park
Ayr.

My Favourite
STORIES OF
SCOTLAND

edited by
JOHN LAURIE

with line decorations by
DOUGLAS PHILLIPS

LUTTERWORTH PRESS
GUILDFORD AND LONDON

Set in 12/12 point Bembo

Printed in Great Britain by
Ebenezer Baylis and Son Ltd
The Trinity Press, Worcester, and London

Contents

CONTENTS

Acknowledgments

The editor and the publishers are indebted to all those who have given permission for the use of material which is their copyright, or who have helped in the obtaining of that permission:

Yale University and William Heinemann Limited, for the extracts from James Boswell's London Journal

Macdonald Publishers, for 'Embro to the Ploy', from *Collected Poems* by Robert Garioch

Mr Fred Urquhart, for the short story 'Mrs Coolie-Hoo's Pole'

Collins (Publishers), for 'The Football Match', from *The Shipbuilders* by George Blake

The Estate of the late Dr Neil Munro, and the Editor of Blackwood's Magazine, for 'The Fell Sergeant'

Curtis Brown Limited, for 'The Long Walk', from *A Skinful of Scotch* by Clifford Hanley

Foreword

Actors as men-of-letters are rare birds; not counting that army of ghosts who haunt stage memoirs I can remember a mere handful. So when out of the blue I was invited to compile this anthology, I accepted with carefree alacrity.

It helped though that I'd given houseroom to far too many books, and that among them were most of those which, after much cogitation, are listed below as my personal choice of good Scots writing. The choosing had its painful moments. Some writers once loved no longer survived the test of a re-read in pernickety old age. John Galt, for instance, now seems cosy and dull. Hogg's *Justified Sinner* is truly as thrilling as ever, but it is unusable because it defies cutting. Stevenson echoes Scott, but too faintly. Barrie's non-dramatic work is more and more unacceptably sentimental these hard times. This applies also to the many stories buried in the dusty volumes of *Blackwood's* and *Frazer's* mid-Victorian magazines; I find their comic tales unfunny and their horrors plain daft.

There's one missing entry that I deeply regret—Robert Henryson's *Testament of Cresseid*. This great narrative poem has haunted me for sixty years; but the generation gap between it and us is too wide. Today the lady speaks a language which only a student of fifteenth-century literature can properly understand. So farewell Cresseid.

The paragraphs that follow are not intended to gloss, still less to justify, each entry. They are no more than introductions to you, the Reader, of a few of my old friends as they fare forth in, I hope, congenial company.

★ ★ ★ ★ ★

A ballad comes first, and that's as it should be. Ballads were there before Caxton; they are the poems a Border Scot would hear in lieu of nursery rhymes. *Edward* is just one of many that I have loved, and spoken. The story of mother, son and dead father is older than Athens. As here printed, it is an eighteenth-century collector's version of a ballad as sung by the last of a long line of singers; that collector was certainly a poet in his own right—he may well have been my next author.

To me the rediscovery of Sir Walter Scott's *Wandering Willie's Tale* was a rare pleasure—I'd forgotten how splendid it is, though I had small excuse. It has often been reprinted since it first appeared in *Redgauntlet*, a fine novel which tells how Prince Charlie—no longer young or bonnie—fails to inspire a third Jacobite rising. Old Willie's tale of Major Weir the jackanapes (think of him as a larger, fiercer organ-grinder's monkey) is both macabre and comic, and told in Scott's ripest Doric. When Sir Walter is in form there's none riper.

James Boswell's London Journal was written for his own pleasure and posted weekly to an Edinburgh friend with no thought that it would be published for all the world to read. It nearly wasn't, for it is barely fifty years since it was discovered mouldering in the attic of a Scottish castle. The entries here printed cover three themes: Boswell's journey south, his settling in London (which includes his vain attempt at securing a commission in the Guards, and his liaison with Mrs Lewis), and, mentioned almost in passing, his regard for Samuel Johnson's work and his eagerness to meet him.

Although Boswell's hope of seeing Johnson at Davies's on Christmas Day, 1762, came to nothing, five months later, on May 16, 1763, he was able to record what matters most of all—his introduction to 'the great Mr Samuel Johnson': a very big, sore-eyed man, troubled by palsy, marked by scrofula, dressed like a sloven, with an uncouth way of speech. 'A most dreadful appearance,' wrote Boswell: but added, 'Yet his great knowledge and strength of expression command vast respect and render him very excellent company.' He did not care for Johnson's dogmatic manners, and Johnson, in his turn, did not care for Boswell's provenance, disliking the Scots intensely. 'Indeed I come from Scotland,' Boswell admitted, 'but I cannot help it.' 'Sir,' Johnson told him, 'that, I find, is what a very great many of your countrymen cannot help.' The remark, faithfully set down, was to open an invaluable record of Johnson's conversations.

The friendship recorded in the entries for December, 1762, is less exalted by far, but it does clarify the darker places in Boswell's character. Louisa Lewis acts as the catalyst: she was an actress of some importance—that autumn Covent Garden had seen her as Hamlet's mother and Falstaff's Mistress Ford. Modesty alas forbids our telling the whole story with its unhappy denouement, for the wretched Boswell contracted the occupational disease of many another eighteenth-century gallant; his subsequent treatment of Louisa makes sad reading. He caps it by demanding repayment by return of the two guineas he had eagerly loaned her six weeks previously. 'I give you notice that I expect to have it before Saturday sennight. I have nothing more to say to you.' She sent his money back without a word. Boswell was momentarily touched, but quickly recovered. 'I was glad,' he said, 'that I'd come off two guineas better than I expected.'

Thomas Carlyle could not have known about Louisa, but his estimate of Boswell, from a review of a forgotten edition of the *Life of Johnson*, has venom enough to avenge her poor ghost. The review was written the year *The French Revolution* was published, with the Sage in full involuted spate and that is how I like him best. Carlyle's judgment may be harsh, but how satisfyingly it fits in, just here!

His wife, Jane Welsh Carlyle, is emerging more and more these days as the great man's co-equal, almost entirely on the literary quality of her letters. Three thousand of them have so far been published, and many more are promised. Incidentally, the most recent collection is significantly titled *I Too Am Here*. Dickens, among others, regretted the novels she never got round to writing. 'None of the writing women come near her at all,' said he. What is here reprinted isn't a letter. It is part of a 'very interesting narrative' (her husband's description) written for the joy of writing—and remembering. It tells us more about this most lovable lady than any letter. Certainly her clever husband could never have seen comedy and pathos in a dumb yokel chewing his cap. Or have risen at dawn to climb a churchyard wall (and in a Victorian skirt too!). Or felt the agenbite of inwit at sight of the old ones and the streets of Haddington: the memories of a happy girlhood and of the dead days.

Dr John Brown's *Rab and his Friends* is as sentimental a story in its way as any in the old *Blackwood's*. The Edinburgh physician, though, had a touch of genius and good taste which raise him above his contemporaries. I wish I hadn't just realized that *Rab* has all the sure-fire ingredients for a successful television serial —a handsome young doctor, a dog, ugly but lovable, and two doomed geriatrics. I still think it's a great yarn.

There's a toast often drunk on Burns' Nichts which goes: 'Here's tae us! Wha's like us?' Unfortunately, many of us begin to believe it, and it is a blot on much Scots writing that it fosters the delusion, thereby inducing instant nausea in all modest Caledonians. In George Douglas Brown's case it evoked a grim and savage counterblast, his novel *The House with the Green Shutters*. 'The kindly kailyard is a lie,' it seems to say. 'Here is our real small-town Scot: wha indeed *is* like us?' The book offended, and it was meant to. It is black comedy with deeply tragic undertones. I count it a happy chance that it is possible to encapsulate so many of the qualities of this great book in these two short chapters.

At this point it seemed that another poem was overdue, to relieve the rhythm of solid prose and to lighten its gloom. Robert Garioch does both most satisfactorily. This poem too is a satire, but of a quality so light-hearted throughout that its very title, *Embro to the Ploy*, sets the mood precisely. Scotland's historic capital dwindles from four rolling syllables to a perky two: its million-dollar Festival of all the Arts re-defined by a homely little word which, in my young days, implied a piece of mischief likely to be committed by an idle wee deil: lastly the English would say '*at* the ploy' and so would lose a Scots nuance. All this glossing of a simple four-word title justifies my decision not to print at the bottom of each page a column of foreign words crudely translated. I am assuming rather that most of Garioch will be easily apprehended by any bright Sassenach who is capable of enjoying his own 'new' poetry—apart, perhaps, from a few 'difficult' words. Here they are: 'eydent' means 'eager'; 'fu sturrit in a steir' is 'greatly stirred in a commotion'; 'suppit puirshous leir' is 'fed on poorhouse learning'; if you 'coup the creel' you upset the applecart (a basket, in this case); 'bawrs' are jokes and 'bields' means shelters. The rest need only intelligent surmise. It's nice to know that the poem will look its shapely self unmarred by dangling distractions.

Our third Edinburgh writer, Fred Urquhart, is very much an authors' author. His fellow writers have praised him as a contemporary Hogarth, with 'a remarkable talent for depicting women, young and old', and that's true. I admire most, though, the living speech of those women, with never a sniff of Dr Jamieson's Scottish Dictionary, so beloved by the Lallans lads. Thank you, Fred. By the way, our author was a wee bit uncertain as to the origin of that lovely word, 'Coolie-Hoo'; could it be, said he, an Urquhart family invention? Alas no. Chambers Scots Dialect Dictionary tells us that 'coolie' means a night cap and 'hoo' also means a night-cap. So the lady was wearing one of those unbecoming pull-on woollie head-covers so favoured by skiers.

There are thousands of Scotsmen for whom Saturday afternoon means one thing—fitba'. It so happens that a shining bit of rapportage in the middle of George Blake's fine novel *The Shipbuilders* deals with the ninety minutes most of them would love to see. They call it the Auld Firm—Celtic *v.* Rangers. Blake loved Glasgow, that dour city, and must have shivered many an hour on the terraces to watch its dourest contest. There's more than a game here, there's a wee bit of Scotland itself.

Sandwiched between two different examples of good realistic writing, serious and comic, comes a tale from north of the Highland line. *The Fell Sergeant*, for all its starkness, lies in that twilight zone between prose and poetry. Reminiscent of J. M. Synge both in setting and language, it has the qualities of his great one-act plays. The climax is delayed most admirably until the last line: a typical bit of Neil Munro magic.

I'm admitting, before I'm found out, that Cliff Hanley and I are old friends. Indeed, I love the man. He put me up one Hogmanay, and I found out that the extravaganzas he chronicles so entertainingly really do happen when he's thereabouts. It delights me that he is here to prove to any doubting Sassenach that there's one Scot who just might make you laugh out loud.

* * * * *

I doubt there's been too much Foreword: less would have left room for another story or poem or essay, and goodness knows there's plenty in reserve: Burns himself, Allan Cunningham, George Macdonald, Crockett, Cunningham Grahame, George Mackay Brown, Linklater, Bridie, Iain Hamilton (another friend),

Stevenson (of course), plus that author whom you, dear Reader, are shocked and disgusted I've left out. Add them up, and there's a Second Eleven which might conceivably beat my First Eleven by a single goal. But I don't believe it.

I need hardly add that any thought of listing my selections in the order they were written was quickly abandoned. A metaphysically superior arrangement prevailed. The ballad and Scott, for example, provided a solid foundation for which that fribble Boswell was quite inadequate. Carlyle arrived on cue to perform a hatchet job, and his Jane followed with her human touch, human enough to prepare the way for the over-tender trap of Rab and his friends. The rest—the great Douglas Brown, Robert Garioch, Fred Urquhart, George Blake, Neil Munro and Cliff Hanley—sorted themselves out with almost no help at all. I hope nothing was lost and a little something gained by this fanciful arrangement.

P.S. On page 7 there is an 'official' list of acknowledgments. I have, personally, three more to add. To Mr Ian Lavender for giving me the photograph used on the back of the jacket of this book, and to Mr Michael Fresco for taking it. To Miss Jenny Overton of the Lutterworth Press for bringing order out of chaos with firmness and kindness far beyond the call of duty. My loving thanks.

J.L.

Edward

AUTHOR UNKNOWN

'Why does your brand sae drop wi' blude,
    Edward, Edward?
Why does your brand sae drop wi' blude,
    And why sae sad gang ye, O?'
'O I hae kill'd my hawk sae gude,
    Mither, mither;
O I hae kill'd my hawk sae gude,
    And I had nae mair but he, O.'

'Your hawk's blude was never sae red,
    Edward, Edward;
Your hawk's blude was never sae red,
    My dear son, I tell thee, O.'
'O I hae kill'd my red-roan steed,
    Mither, mither;
O I hae kill'd my red-roan steed,
    That erst was sae fair and free, O.'

'Your steed was auld, and ye hae got mair,
    Edward, Edward;
Your steed was auld, and ye hae got mair;
    Some other dule ye dree, O.'
'O I hae kill'd my father dear,
    Mither, mither;
O I hae kill'd my father dear,
    Alas, and wae is me, O!'

'And whatten penance will ye dree for that,
    Edward, Edward?
Whatten penance will ye dree for that?
    My dear son, now tell me, O.'
'*I'll set my feet in yonder boat,*
    Mither, mither;
I'll set my feet in yonder boat,
    And I'll fare over the sea, O.'

'And what will ye do wi' your tow'rs and your ha',
    Edward, Edward?
And what will ye do wi' your tow'rs and your ha',
    That were sae fair to see, O?'
'*I'll let them stand till they doun fa',*
    Mither, mither;
I'll let them stand till they doun fa',
    For here never mair maun I be, O.'

'And what will ye leave to your bairns and your wife,
    Edward, Edward?
And what will ye leave to your bairns and your wife,
    When ye gang owre the sea, O?'
'*The warld's room: let them beg through life,*
    Mither, mither;
The warld's room: let them beg through life;
    For them never mair will I see, O.'

'And what will ye leave to your ain mither dear,
    Edward, Edward?
And what will ye leave to your ain mither dear,
    My dear son, now tell me, O?'
'*The curse of hell frae me sall ye bear,*
    Mither, mither;
The curse of hell frae me sall ye bear;
    Sic counsels ye gave to me, O!'

2

Wandering Willie's Tale

SIR WALTER SCOTT

Ye maun have heard of Sir Robert Redgauntlet of that Ilk, who lived in these parts before the dear years. The country will lang mind him; and our fathers used to draw breath thick if ever they heard him named. He was out wi' the Hielandmen in Montrose's time; and again he was in the hills wi' Glencairn in the saxteen hundred and fifty-twa; and sae when King Charles the Second came in, wha was in sic favour as the Laird of Redgauntlet? He was knighted at Lonon court, wi' the king's ain sword; and being a redhot prelatist, he came down here, rampauging like a lion, with commissions of lieutenancy (and of lunacy, for what I ken) to put down a' the Whigs and Covenanters in the country. Wild wark they made of it; for the Whigs were as dour as the Cavaliers were fierce, and it was which should first tire the other. Redgauntlet was ay for the strong hand; and his name is kend as wide in the country as Claverhouse's or Tam Dalyell's. Glen, nor dargle, nor mountain, nor cave, could hide the puir hill-folk when Redgauntlet was out with bugle and bloodhound after them, as if they had been sae mony deer. And troth when they fand them, they didna mak muckle mair ceremony than a Hielandman wi' a roebuck—it was just, 'Will ye tak the test?'— if not, 'Make ready—present—fire!'—and there lay the recusant.

Far and wide was Sir Robert hated and feared. Men thought he had a direct compact with Satan—that he was proof against steel —and that bullets happed aff his buff-coat like hailstanes from a hearth—that he had a mear that would turn a hare on the side of Carrifra-gawns—and muckle to the same purpose, of whilk mair anon. The best blessing they wared on him was, 'Deil scowp wi' Redgauntlet!' He wasna a bad master to his ain folk, though, and was weel aneugh liked by his tenants; and as for the lackies and troopers that raid out wi' him to the persecutions, as the Whigs caa'd those killing times, they wad hae drunken themsells blind to his health at ony time.

Now you are to ken that my gudesire lived on Redgauntlet's grund—they ca' the place Primrose Knowe. We had lived on the grund, and under the Redgauntlets, since the riding days, and lang before. It was a pleasant bit; and I think the air is callerer and fresher there than onywhere else in the country. It's a' deserted now; and I sat on the broken door-cheek three days since, and was glad I couldna see the plight the place was in; but that's a' wide o' the mark. There dwelt my gudesire, Steenie Steenson, a rambling, rattling chiel' he had been in his young days, and could play weel on the pipes; he was famous at 'Hoopers and Girders'—a' Cumberland couldna touch him at 'Jockie Lattin'— and he had the finest finger for the back-lilt between Berwick and Carlisle. The like o' Steenie wasna the sort that they made Whigs o'. And so he became a Tory, as they ca' it, which we now ca' Jacobites, just out of a kind of needcessity, that he might belang to some side or other. He had nae ill will to the Whig bodies, and liked little to see the blude rin, though, being obliged to follow Sir Robert in hunting and hoisting, watching and warding, he saw muckle mischief, and maybe did some, that he couldna avoid.

Now Steenie was a kind of favourite with his master, and kend a' the folks about the castle, and was often sent for to play the pipes when they were at their merriment. Auld Dougal Mac-Callum, the butler, that had followed Sir Robert through gude and ill, thick and thin, pool and stream, was specially fond of the pipes, and ay gae my gudesire his gude word wi' the laird; for Dougal could turn his master round his finger.

Weel, round came the Revolution, and it had like to have broken the hearts baith of Dougal and his master. But the change was not a'thegether sae great as they feared, and other folk thought for. The Whigs made an unco crawing what they wad do with their auld enemies, and in special wi' Sir Robert Red-gauntlet. But there were ower mony great folks dipped in the same doings, to mak a spick and span new warld. So Parliament passed it a' ower easy; and Sir Robert, bating that he was held to hunting foxes instead of Covenanters, remained just the man he was. His revel was as loud, and his hall as weel lighted, as ever it had been, though maybe he lacked the fines of the non-conformists, that used to come to stock his larder and cellar; for it is certain he began to be keener about the rents than his tenants used to find him before, and they behoved to be prompt to the rent-day, or else the laird wasna pleased. And he was sic an awsome body, that naebody cared to anger him; for the oaths he swore, and the rages that he used to get into, and the looks that he put on, made men sometimes think him a devil incarnate.

Weel, my gudesire was nae manager—no' that he was a very great misguider—but he hadna the saving gift, and he got twa terms' rent in arrear. He got the first brash at Whitsunday put ower wi' fair word and piping; but when Martinmas came, there was a summons from the grund-officer to come wi' the rent on a day preceese, or else Steenie behoved to flit. Sair wark he had to get the siller; but he was weel-freended, and at last he got the haill scraped thegether—a thousand merks—the maist of it was from a neighbour they ca'd Laurie Lapraik—a sly tod. Laurie had walth o' gear—could hunt wi' the hound and rin wi' the hare—and be Whig or Tory, saunt or sinner, as the wind stood. He was a professor in this Revolution warld, but he liked an orra sough of this warld, and a tune on the pipes weel aneugh at a bytime; and abune a', he thought he had gude security for the siller he lent my gudesire ower the stocking at Primrose Knowe.

Away trots my gudesire to Redgauntlet Castle wi' a heavy purse and a light heart, glad to be out of the laird's danger. Weel, the first thing he learned at the castle was, that Sir Robert had fretted himsell into a fit of the gout, because he did not appear before twelve o'clock. It wasna a'thegether for sake of the money, Dougal thought; but because he didna like to part wi' my gude-sire aff the grund. Dougal was glad to see Steenie, and brought him into the great oak parlour, and there sat the laird his leesome lane, excepting that he had beside him a great, ill-favoured jackanape, that was a special pet of his; a cankered beast it was, and mony an ill-natured trick it played—ill to please it was, and easily angered—ran about the haill castle, chattering and yowling, and pinching, and biting folk, specially before ill weather, or disturbances in the state. Sir Robert caa'd it 'Major Weir', after the warlock that was burnt; and few folk liked either the name or the conditions of the creature—they thought there was something in it by ordinar—and my gudesire was not just easy in mind when the door shut on him, and he saw himself in the room wi' naebody but the laird, Dougal MacCallum, and the Major, a thing that hadna chanced to him before.

Sir Robert sat, or, I should say, lay, in a great armed chair, wi' his grand velvet gown, and his feet on a cradle; for he had baith gout and gravel, and his face looked as gash and ghastly as Satan's. Major Weir sat opposite to him, in a red laced coat, and the laird's wig on his head; and ay as Sir Robert girned wi' pain, the jackanape girned too, like a sheep's-head between a pair of tangs—an aill-faur'd, fearsome couple they were. The laird's buff-coat was hung on a pin behind him, and his broadsword and his pistols within reach; for he keepit up the auld fashion of having the weapons ready, and a horse saddled day and night, just as he used to do when he was able to loup on horseback, and away after ony of the hill-folk he could get speerings of. Some said it was for fear of the Whigs taking vengeance, but I judge it was just his auld custom—he wasna gien to fear onything. The rental-book, wi' its black cover and brass clasps, was lying beside him; and a book of sculduddry sangs was put betwixt the leaves, to keep it open at the place where it bore evidence against the Goodman of Primrose Knowe, as behind the hand with his mails and duties. Sir Robert gave my gudesire a look, as if he would have withered his heart in his bosom. Ye maun ken he had a way of bending his brows, that men saw the visible mark of a horse-shoe in his forehead, deep dinted, as if it had been stamped there.

'Are ye come light-handed, ye son of a toom whistle?' said Sir Robert. 'Zounds! if you are——'

My gudesire, with as gude a countenance as he could put on, made a leg, and placed the bag of money on the table wi' a dash, like a man that does something clever. The laird drew it to him hastily—'Is it all here, Steenie, man?'

'Your honour will find it right,' said my gudesire.

'Here, Dougal,' said the laird, 'gie Steenie a tass of brandy downstairs, till I count the siller and write the receipt.'

But they werena weel out of the room, when Sir Robert gied a yelloch that garr'd the castle rock. Back ran Dougal—in flew the livery-men—yell on yell gied the laird, ilk ane mair awfu' than the ither. My gudesire knew not whether to stand or flee, but he ventured back into the parlour, where a' was gaun hirdygirdie—naebody to say 'come in', or 'gae out'. Terribly the laird roared for cauld water to his feet, and wine to cool his throat; and Hell, hell, hell, and its flames, was ay the word in his mouth. They brought him water, and when they plunged his swollen feet into the tub, he cried out it was burning; and folk say that it *did* bubble and sparkle like a seething cauldron. He flung the cup at Dougal's head, and said he had given him blood instead of burgundy; and, sure aneugh, the lass washed clotted blood aff the carpet the neist day. The jackanape they caa'd Major Weir, it jibbered and cried as if it was mocking its master; my gudesire's head was like to turn—he forgot baith siller and receipt, and downstairs he banged; but as he ran, the shrieks came faint and fainter; there was a deep-drawn shivering groan, and word gaed through the castle that the laird was dead.

Weel, away came my gudesire, wi' his finger in his mouth, and his best hope was that Dougal had seen the moneybag, and heard the laird speak of writing the receipt. The young laird, now Sir John, came from Edinburgh, to see things put to rights. Sir John and his father never gree'd weel. Sir John had been bred an advocate, and afterwards sat in the last Scots Parliament and voted for the Union, having gotten, it was thought, a rug of the compensations—if his father could have come out of his grave, he would have brained him for it on his awn hearthstane. Some thought it was easier counting with the auld rough knight than the fair-spoken young ane—but mair of that anon.

Dougal MacCallum, poor body, neither grat nor grained, but gaed about the house looking like a corpse, but directing, as was his duty, a' the order of the grand funeral. Now, Dougal looked ay waur and waur when night was coming, and was ay the last to gang to his bed, whilk was in a little round just opposite the chamber of dais, whilk his master occupied while he was living, and where he now lay in state, as they caa'd it, weel-a-day! The night before the funeral, Dougal could keep his awn counsel nae langer; he came doun with his proud spirit, and fairly asked auld Hutcheon to sit in his room with him for an hour. When they were in the round, Dougal took ae tass of brandy to himsell, and gave another to Hutcheon, and wished him all health and lang life, and said that, for himsell, he wasna lang for this world; for that, every night since Sir Robert's death, his silver call had sounded from the state chamber, just as it used to do at nights in his lifetime, to call Dougal to help to turn him in his bed. Dougal said that being alone with the dead on that floor of the tower (for naebody cared to wake Sir Robert Redgauntlet like another corpse) he had never daured to answer the call, but that now his conscience checked him for neglecting his duty; for, 'though death breaks service,' said MacCallum, 'it shall never break my service to Sir Robert; and I will answer his next whistle, so be you will stand by me, Hutcheon.'

Hutcheon had nae will to the wark, but he had stood by Dougal in battle and broil, and he wad not fail him at this pinch; so down the carles sat ower a stoup of brandy, and Hutcheon, who was something of a clerk, would have read a chapter of the Bible; but Dougal would hear naething but a blaud of Davie Lindsay, whilk was the waur preparation.

When midnight came, and the house was quiet as the grave, sure enough the silver whistle sounded as sharp and shrill as if Sir Robert was blawing it, and up got the twa auld serving-men, and tottered into the room where the dead man lay. Hutcheon saw aneugh at the first glance; for there were torches in the room, which showed him the foul fiend, in his ain shape, sitting on the laird's coffin! Ower he cowped as if he had been dead. He could not tell how lang he lay in a trance at the door, but when he gathered himsell, he cried on his neighbour, and getting nae answer, raised the house, when Dougal was found lying dead within twa steps of the bed where his master's coffin was placed. As for the whistle, it was gaen anes and ay; but mony a time was it heard at the top of the house on the bartizan, and amang the auld chimneys and turrets where the howlets have their nests. Sir John hushed the matter up, and the funeral passed over without mair bogle-wark.

But when a' was ower, and the laird was beginning to settle his affairs, every tenant was called up for his arrears, and my gudesire for the full sum that stood against him in the rental-book. Weel, away he trots to the castle, to tell his story, and there he is introduced to Sir John, sitting in his father's chair, in deep mourning, with weepers and hanging cravat, and a small walking rapier by his side, instead of the auld broadsword that had a hundredweight of steel about it, what with blade, chape, and basket-hilt. I have heard their communing so often tauld ower, that I almost think I was there mysell, though I couldna be born at the time.

(In fact, my companion mimicked, with a good deal of humour, the flattering, conciliating tone of the tenant's address, and the hypocritical melancholy of the laird's reply. His grandfather, he said, had, while he spoke, his eye fixed on the rental-book, as if it were a mastiff-dog that he was afraid would spring up and bite him.)

'I wuss ye joy, sir, of the head seat, and the white loaf, and the braid lairdship. Your father was a kind man to friends and followers; muckle grace to you, Sir John, to fill his shoon—his boots, I suld say, for he seldom wore shoon, unless it were muils when he had the gout.'

'Aye, Steenie,' quoth the laird, sighing deeply, and putting his napkin to his een, 'his was a sudden call, and he will be missed in the country; no time to set his house in order—weel prepared Godward, no doubt, which is the root of the matter—but left us behind a tangled hesp to wind, Steenie.——Hem! hem! We maun go to business, Steenie; much to do, and little time to do it in.'

Here he opened the fatal volume. I have heard of a thing they call Doomsday Book—I am clear it has been a rental of back-ganging tenants.

'Stephen,' said Sir John, still in the same soft, sleekit tone of voice—'Stephen Stevenson, or Steenson, ye are down here for a year's rent behind the hand—due at last term.'

Stephen. 'Please your honour, Sir John, I paid it to your father.'

Sir John. 'Ye took a receipt, then, doubtless, Stephen; and can produce it?'

Stephen. 'Indeed I hadna time, an it like your honour; for nae sooner had I set doun the siller, and just as his honour, Sir Robert, that's gaen, drew it till him to count it, and write out the receipt, he was ta'en wi' the pains that removed him.'

'That was unlucky,' said Sir John, after a pause. 'But ye maybe paid it in the presence of somebody. I want but a *talis qualis* evidence, Stephen. I would go ower strictly to work with no poor man.'

Stephen. 'Troth, Sir John, there was naebody in the room but Dougal MacCallum the butler. But, as your honour kens, he has e'en followed his auld master.'

'Very unlucky again, Stephen,' said Sir John, without altering his voice a single note. 'The man to whom ye paid the money is

dead—and the man who witnessed the payment is dead too—
and the siller, which should have been to the fore, is neither seen
nor heard tell of in the repositories. How am I to believe a' this?'

Stephen. 'I dinna ken, your honour; but there is a bit memor-
andum note of the very coins; for, God help me! I had to borrow
out of twenty purses; and I am sure that ilka man there set down
will take his grit oath for what purpose I borrowed the money.'

Sir John. 'I have little doubt ye *borrowed* the money, Steenie.
It is the *payment* to my father that I want to have some proof of.'

Stephen. 'The siller maun be about the house, Sir John. And
since your honour never got it, and his honour that was canna
have taen it wi' him, maybe some of the family may have seen it.'

Sir John. 'We will examine the servants, Stephen; that is but
reasonable.'

But lackey and lass, and page and groom, all denied stoutly
that they had ever seen such a bag of money as my gudesire
described. What was waur, he had unluckily not mentioned to
any living soul of them his purpose of paying his rent. Ae quean
had noticed something under his arm, but she took it for the pipes.

Sir John Redgauntlet ordered the servants out of the room, and
then said to my gudesire, 'Now, Steenie, ye see ye have fair play;
and, as I have little doubt ye ken better where to find the siller
than ony other body, I beg, in fair terms, and for your own sake,
that you will end this fasherie; for, Stephen, ye maun pay or flit.'

'The Lord forgie your opinion,' said Stephen, driven almost
to his wits end—'I am an honest man.'

'So am I, Stephen,' said his honour; 'and so are all the folks
in the house, I hope. But if there be a knave amongst us, it must
be he that tells the story he cannot prove.' He paused, and then
added, mair sternly, 'If I understand your trick, sir, you want to
take advantage of some malicious reports concerning things in
this family, and particularly respecting my father's sudden death,
thereby to cheat me out of the money, and perhaps take away my
character by insinuating that I have received the rent I am demanding. Where do you suppose this money to be? I insist upon
knowing.'

My gudesire saw everything look so muckle against him, that
he grew nearly desperate—however, he shifted from one foot to
another, looked to every corner of the room, and made no
answer.

'Speak out, sirrah,' said the laird, assuming a look of his

father's, a very particular ane, which he had when he was angry
—it seemed as if the wrinkles of his frown made that selfsame
fearful shape of a horse's shoe in the middle of his brow;——
'Speak out, sir! I *will* know your thoughts;—do you suppose
that I have this money?'

'Far be it frae me to say so,' said Stephen.

'Do you charge any of my people with having taken it?'

'I wad be laith to charge them that may be innocent,' said my
gudesire; 'and if there be any one that is guilty, I have nae proof.'

'Somewhere the money must be, if there is a word of truth in
your story,' said Sir John; 'I ask where you think it is—and
demand a correct answer?'

'In hell, if you *will* have my thoughts of it,' said my gudesire,
driven to extremity, 'in hell! with your father, his jackanape, and
his silver whistle.'

Down the stairs he ran (for the parlour was nae place for him
after such a word) and he heard the laird swearing blood and
wounds behind him, as fast as ever did Sir Robert, and roaring
for the bailie and the baron-officer.

Away rode my gudesire to his chief creditor (him they ca'd
Laurie Lapraik) to try if he could make onything out of him;
but when he tauld his story, he got but the worst word in his
wame—thief, beggar, and dyvour, were the saftest terms; and to
the boot of these hard terms, Laurie brought up the auld story of
his dipping his hand in the blood of God's saunts, just as if a
tenant could have helped riding with the laird, and that a laird
like Sir Robert Redgauntlet. My gudesire was, by this time, far
beyond the bounds of patience, and, while he and Laurie were
at deil speed the liars, he was wanchancie aneugh to abuse
Lapraik's doctrine as weel as the man, ond said things that garr'd
folks' flesh grue that heard them;—he wasna just himsell, and he
had lived wi' a wild set in his day.

At last they parted, and my gudesire was to ride hame through
the wood of Pitmurkie, that is a' fou of black firs, as they say.
——I ken the wood, but the firs may be black or white for what
I can tell.——At the entry of the wood there is a wild common,
and on the edge of the common, a little lonely change-house,
that was keepit then by an ostler-wife, they suld hae caa'd her
Tibbie Faw, and there puir Steenie cried for a mutchkin of
brandy, for he had had no refreshment the haill day. Tibbie was
earnest wi' him to take a bite of meat, but he couldna think o't,

nor would he take his foot out of the stirrup, and took off the brandy wholely at twa draughts, and named a toast at each:—the first was the memory of Sir Robert Redgauntlet, and might he never lie quiet in his grave till he had righted his poor bond-tenant; and the second was a health to Man's Enemy, if he would but get him back the pock of siller or tell him what came o't, for he saw the haill world was like to regard him as a thief and a cheat, and he took that waur than even the ruin of his house and hauld.

On he rode, little caring where. It was a dark night turned, and the trees made it yet darker, and he let the beast take its ain road through the wood; when all of a sudden, from tired and wearied that it was before, the nag began to spring and flee, and stend, that my gudesire could hardly keep the saddle. Upon the whilk, a horseman, suddenly riding up beside him, said, 'That's a mettle beast of yours, freend; will you sell him?' So saying, he touched the horse's neck with his riding-wand, and it fell into its auld heigh-ho of a stumbling trot. 'But his spunk's soon out of him, I think,' continued the stranger, 'and that is like mony a man's courage, that thinks he wad do great things till he come to the proof.'

My gudesire scarce listened to this, but spurred his horse, with 'Gude e'en to you, freend.'

But it's like the stranger was ane that doesna lightly yeild his point; for, ride as Steenie liked, he was ay beside him at the selfsame pace. At last my gudesire, Steenie Steenson, grew half angry, and, to say the truth, half feared.

'What is it that ye want with me, freend?' he said. 'If ye be a robber, I have nae money; if ye be a leal man, wanting company, I have nae heart to mirth or speaking; and if ye want to ken the road, I scarce ken it mysell.'

'If you will tell me your grief,' said the stranger, 'I am one that, though I have been sair miscaa'd in the world, am the only hand for helping my freends.'

So my gudesire, to ease his ain heart, mair than from any hope of help, told him the story from beginning to end.

'It's a hard pinch,' said the stranger; 'but I think I can help you.'

'If you could lend me the money, sir, and take a lang day—I ken nae other help on earth,' said my gudesire.

'But there may be some under the earth,' said the stranger. 'Come, I'll be frank wi' you; I could lend you the money on bond, but you would maybe scruple my terms. Now, I can tell you, that your auld laird is disturbed in his grave by your curses, and the wailing of your family, and if ye daur venture to go to see him, he will give you the receipt.'

My gudesire's hair stood on end at this proposal, but he thought his companion might be some humoursome chield that was trying to frighten him, and might end with lending him the money. Besides, he was bauld wi' brandy, and desperate wi' distress; and he said he had courage to go to the gate of hell, and a step farther, for that receipt. The stranger laughed.

Weel, they rode on through the thickest of the wood, when, all of a sudden, the horse stopped at the door of a great house; and, but that he knew the place was ten miles off, my father would have thought he was at Redgauntlet Castle. They rode into the outer courtyard, through the muckle faulding yetts and aneath the auld portcullis; and the whole front of the house was lighted, and there were pipes and fiddles, and as much dancing and deray within as used to be at Sir Robert's house at Pace and Yule, and such high seasons. They lap off, and my gudesire, as seemed to him, fastened his horse to the very ring he had tied him to that morning, when he gaed to wait on the young Sir John.

'God!' said my gudesire, 'if Sir Robert's death be but a dream!'

He knocked at the ha' door just as he was wont, and his auld acquaintance, Dougal MacCallum—just after his wont, too—came to open the door, and said, 'Piper Steenie, are ye there, lad? Sir Robert has been crying for you.'

My gudesire was like a man in a dream—he looked for the stranger, but he was gane for the time. At last he just tried to say, 'Ha! Dougal Driveower, are ye living? I thought ye had been dead.'

'Never fash yoursell wi' me,' said Dougal, 'but look to yoursell; and see ye tak naething frae ony body here, neither meat, drink, or siller, except just the receipt that is your ain.'

So saying, he led the way out through halls and trances that were weel kend to my gudesire, and into the auld oak parlour; and there was as much singing of profane sangs, and birling of red wine, and speaking blasphemy and sculduddry, as had ever been in Redgauntlet Castle when it was at the blithest.

But, Lord take us in keeping, what a set of ghastly revellers they were that sat around that table! My gudesire kend mony that had long before gane to their place, for often had he piped to

the most part in the hall of Redgauntlet. There was the fierce
Middleton, and the dissolute Rothes, and the crafty Lauderdale;
and Dalyell, with his bald head and a beard to his girdle; and
Earlshall, with Cameron's blude on his hand; and wild Bonshaw,
that tied blessed Mr Cargill's limbs till the blude sprung; and
Dunbarton Douglas, the twice-turned traitor baith to country
and king. There was the Bluidy Advocate MacKenyie, who for
his worldly wit and wisdom had been to the rest as a god. And
there was Claverhouse, as beautiful as when he lived, with his
long, dark, curled locks streaming down over his laced buff-coat,
and his left hand always on his right spule-blade, to hide the wound
that the silver bullet had made. He sat apart from them all, and
looked at them with a melancholy, haughty countenance; while
the rest hallooed, and sang, and laughed, that the room rang. But
their smiles were fearfully contorted from time to time; and their
laugh passed into such wild sounds as made my gudesire's very
nails grow blue, and chilled the marrow in his banes.

They that waited at the table were just the wicked serving-men
and troopers, that had done their work and cruel bidding on
earth. There was the Lang Lad of the Nethertown, that helped
to take Argyle; and the bishop's summoner, that they called the
Deil's Rattle-bag; and the wicked guardsmen in their laced coats;
and the savage Highland Amorites, that shed blood like water;
and mony a proud serving-man, haughty of heart and bloody of
hand, cringing to the rich, and making them wickeder than they
would be; grinding the poor to powder, when the rich had broken
them to fragments. And mony, mony mair were coming and
ganging, a' as busy in their vocation as if they had been alive.

Sir Robert Redgauntlet, in the midst of a' this fearful riot,
cried, wi' a voice like thunder, on Steenie Piper to come to the
board-head where he was sitting; his legs stretched out before him,
and swathed up with flannel, with his holster pistols aside him,
while the great broadsword rested against his chair, just as my
gudesire had seen him the last time upon earth—the very cushion
for the jackanape was close to him, but the creature itself was not
there—it wasna its hour, it's likely; for he heard them say as he
came forward, 'Is not the Major come yet?' And another answered
'The jackanape will be here betimes the morn.' And when my
gudesire came forward, Sir Robert, or his ghaist, or the deevil in
his likeness, said, 'Weel, piper, hae ye settled wi' my son for
the year's rent?'

With much ado my father gat breath to say that Sir John would not settle without his honour's receipt.

'Ye shall hae that for a tune of the pipes, Steenie,' said the appearance of Sir Robert—'Play us up "Weel hoddled, Luckie".'

Now this was a tune my gudesire learned frae a warlock, that heard it when they were worshipping Satan at their meetings, and my gudesire had sometimes played it at the ranting suppers in Redgauntlet Castle, but never very willingly; and now he grew cauld at the very name of it, and said, for excuse, he hadna his pipes wi' him.

'MacCallum, ye limb of Beelzebub,' said the fearfu' Sir Robert, 'bring Steenie the pipes that I am keeping for him!'

MacCallum brought a pair of pipes might have served the piper of Donald of the Isles. But he gave my gudesire a nudge as he offered them; and looking secretly and closely, Steenie saw that the chanter was of steel, and heated to a white heat; so he had fair warning not to trust his fingers with it. So he excused himself again, and said he was faint and frightened, and had not wind aneugh to fill the bag.

'Then ye maun eat and drink, Steenie,' said the figure; 'for we do little else here; and it's ill speaking between a fou man and a fasting.'

Now these were the very words that the bloody Earl of Douglas said to keep the king's messenger in hand while he cut the head off MacLellan of Bombie, at the Threave Castle, and that put Steenie mair and mair on his guard. So he spoke up like a man, and said he came neither to eat, or drink, or make minstrelsy; but simply for his ain—to ken what was come o' the money he had paid, and get a discharge for it; and he was so stout-hearted by this time that he charged Sir Robert for conscience-sake (he had no power to say the holy name) and as he hoped for peace and rest, to spread no snares for him, but just to give him his ain.

The appearance gnashed its teeth, and laughed, but it took from a large pocket-book the receipt, and handed it to Steenie. 'There is your receipt, ye pitiful cur; and for the money, my dog-whelp of a son may go look for it in the Cat's Cradle.'

My gudesire uttered mony thanks, and was about to retire when Sir Robert roared aloud, 'Stop, though, thou sack-doudling son of a whore! I am not done with thee. HERE we do nothing for nothing; and you must return on this very day twelvemonth, to pay your master the homage that you owe me for my protection.'

My father's tongue was loosed of a suddenty, and he said aloud, 'I refer mysell to God's pleasure, and not to yours.'

He had no sooner uttered the word than all was dark around him; and he sank on the earth with such a sudden shock, that he lost both breath and sense.

How lang Steenie lay there, he could not tell; but when he came to himself, he was lying in the auld kirkyard of Redgauntlet parochine just at the door of the family aisle, and the scutcheon of the auld knight, Sir Robert, hanging over his head. There was a deep morning fog on grass and gravestane around him, and his horse was feeding quietly beside the minister's twa cows. Steenie would have thought the whole was a dream, but he had the receipt in his hand, fairly written and signed by the auld laird; only the last letters of his name were a little disorderly, written like one seized with sudden pain.

Sorely troubled in his mind, he left that dreary place, rode through the mist to Redgauntlet Castle, and with much ado he got speech of the laird.

'Well, you dyvour bankrupt,' was the first word, 'have you brought me my rent?'

'No,' answered my gudesire, 'I have not; but I have brought your honour Sir Robert's receipt for it.'

'How, sirrah? Sir Robert's receipt! You told me he had not given you one.'

'Will your honour please to see if that bit line is right?'

Sir John looked at every line, and at every letter, with much attention; and, at last, at the date, which my gudesire had not observed—' "From my appointed place," he read, "this twenty-fifth of November."—What!—That is yesterday!—Villain, thou must have gone to hell for this!'

'I got it from your honour's father—whether he be in heaven or hell, I know not,' said Steenie.

'I will delate you for a warlock to the Privy Council!' said Sir John. 'I will send you to your master, the devil, with the help of a tar-barrel and a torch!'

'I intend to delate mysell to the Presbytery,' said Steenie, 'and tell them all I have seen last night, whilk are things fitter for them to judge of than a borrel man like me.'

Sir John paused, composed himsell, and desired to hear the

full history; and my gudesire told it him from point to point, as I have told it you—word for word, neither more nor less.

Sir John was silent again for a long time, and at last he said, very composedly, 'Steenie, this story of yours concerns the honour of many a noble family besides mine; and if it be a leasing-making, to keep yourself out of my danger, the least you can expect is to have a redhot iron driven through your tongue, and that will be as bad as scauding your fingers wi' a redhot chanter. But yet it may be true, Steenie; and if the money cast up, I shall not know what to think of it. But where shall we find the Cat's Cradle? There are cats enough about the old house, but I think they kitten without the ceremony of bed or cradle.'

'We were best ask Hutcheon,' said my gudesire; 'he kens a' the odd corners about as weel as—another serving-man that is now gane, and that I wad not like to name.'

Aweel, Hutcheon, when he was asked, told them that a ruinous turret, lang disused, next to the clock-house, only accessible by a ladder, for the opening was on the outside, and far above the battlements, was called of old 'the Cat's Cradle'.

'There will I go immediately,' said Sir John; and he took (with what purpose, Heaven kens) one of his father's pistols from the hall-table, where they had lain since the night he died, and hastened to the battlements.

It was a dangerous place to climb, for the ladder was auld and frail, and wanted ane or twa rounds. However, up got Sir John, and entered at the turret-door, where his body stopped the only little light that was in the bit turret. Something flees at him wi' a vengeance, maist dang him back ower—bang gaed the knight's pistol, and Hutcheon, that held the ladder, and my gudesire, that stood beside him, hears a loud skelloch. A minute after, Sir John flings the body of the jackanape down to them, and cries that the siller is fund, and that they should come up and help him. And there was the bag of siller sure aneugh, and mony orra thing besides, that had been missing for mony a day. And Sir John, when he had riped the turret weel, led my gudesire into the dining-parlour, and took him by the hand and spoke kindly to him, and said he was sorry he should have doubted his word and that he would hereafter be a good master to him to make amends.

'And now, Steenie,' said Sir John, 'although this vision of yours tend, on the whole, to my father's credit, as an honest man, that he should, even after his death, desire to see justice done to a poor man like you, yet you are sensible that ill-dispositioned men might make bad constructions upon it, concerning his soul's health. So, I think, we had better lay the haill dirdum on that ill-deedie creature, Major Weir, and say naething about your dream in the wood of Pitmurkie. You had taken ower muckle brandy to be very certain about onything; and, Steenie, this receipt' (his hand shook while he held it out),—'it's but a queer kind of document, and we will do best, I think, to put it quietly in the fire.'

'Od, but for as queer as it is, it's a' the voucher I have for my rent,' said my gudesire, who was afraid, it may be, of losing the benefit of Sir Robert's discharge.

'I will bear the contents to your credit in the rental-book, and give you a discharge under my own hand,' said Sir John, 'and that on the spot. And, Steenie, if you can hold your tongue about this matter, you shall sit, from this term downward, at an easier rent.'

'Mony thanks to your honour,' said Steenie, who saw easily in what corner the wind was; 'doubtless I will be comfortable to all your honour's commands; only I would willingly speak wi' some powerful minister on the subject, for I do not like the sort of soumons of appointment whilk your honour's father—'

'Do not call the phantom my father!' said Sir John, interrupting him.

'Well, then, the thing that was so like him,' said my gudesire; 'he spoke of my coming back to see him this time twelvemonth, and it's a weight on my conscience.'

'Aweel, then,' said Sir John, 'if you be so much distressed in mind, you may speak to our minister of the parish; he is a douce man, regards the honour of our family, and the mair that he may look for some patronage from me.'

Wi' that, my father readily agreed that the receipt should be burnt, and the laird threw it into the chimney with his ain hand. Burn it would not for them, though; but away it flew up the lum, wi' a lang train of sparks at its tail, and a hissing noise like a squib.

My gudesire gaed down to the Manse, and the minister, when he had heard the story, said it was his real opinion that though my gudesire had gaen very far in tampering with dangerous matters, yet, as he had refused the devil's arles (for such was the offer of meat and drink) and had refused to do homage by piping at his bidding, he hoped that if he held a circumspect walk hereafter, Satan could take little advantage by what was come and gane. And, indeed, my gudesire, of his ain accord, lang foreswore baith the pipes and the brandy—it was not even till the year was out, and the fatal day past, that he would so much as take the fiddle, or drink usquebaugh or tippeny.

Sir John made up his story about the jackanape as he liked himsell; and some believe till this day there was no more in the matter than the filching nature of the brute. Indeed, ye'll no hinder some to threap that it was nane o' the auld Enemy that Dougal and Hutcheon saw in the laird's room, but only that wanchancy creature, the major, capering on the coffin; and that, as to the blawing on the laird's whistle that was heard after he was dead, the filthy brute could do that as weel as the laird himsell, if no better. But Heaven kens the truth, whilk first came out by the minister's wife, after Sir John and her ain gudeman were baith in the moulds. And then my gudesire, who was failed in his limbs, but not in his judgment or memory—at least nothing to speak of—was obliged to tell the real narrative to his friends, for the credit of his good name. He might else have been charged for a warlock.

A Scotsman On The Make

JAMES BOSWELL'S LONDON JOURNAL

1762

Monday 15 November. Elated with the thoughts of my journey to London, I got up. I called upon my friend Johnston, but found he was not come from the country, which vexed me a little, as I wished to bid him cordially adieu. However, I excused him to myself, and as Cairnie told me that people never took leave in France, I made the thing sit pretty easy. I had a long serious conversation with my father and mother. They were very kind to me. I felt parental affection was very strong towards me; and I felt a very warm filial regard for them. The scene of being a son setting out from home for the wide world and the idea of being my own master, pleased me much. I parted with my brother Davy, leaving him my best advices to be diligent at his business as a banker and to make rich and be happy.

At ten I got into my chaise, and away I went. As I passed the Cross, the cadies and the chairmen bowed and seemed to say, 'GOD prosper long our noble Boswell.' I rattled down the High Street in high elevation of spirits, bowed and smiled to acquaintances, and took up my partner at Boyd's Close. He was a Mr Stewart, eldest son to Ardsheal, who was forfeited in the year 1746. He had made four voyages to the East Indies, and was now going out first mate. I made the chaise stop at the foot of the Canongate; asked pardon of Mr Stewart for a minute; walked to the Abbey of Holyroodhouse, went round the Piazzas, bowed thrice: once to the Palace itself, once to the crown of Scotland

above the gate in front, and once to the venerable old Chapel. I
next stood in the court before the Palace, and bowed thrice to
Arthur Seat, that lofty romantic mountain on which I have so
often strayed in my days of youth, indulged meditation and felt
the raptures of a soul filled with ideas of the magnificence of GOD
and his creation. Having thus gratified my agreeable whim and
superstitious humour, I felt a warm glow of satisfaction. Indeed,
I have a strong turn to what the cool part of mankind have
named superstition. But this proceeds from my genius for poetry,
which ascribes many fanciful properties to everything. This I
have great pleasure from; as I have now by experience and reflec-
tion gained the command of it so far that I can keep it within
just bounds by the power of reason, without losing the agreeable
feeling and play to the imagination which it bestows. I am
surely much happier in this way than if I just considered Holyroodhouse as so much stone and lime which has been put together
in a certain way, and Arthur Seat as so much earth and rock
raised above the neighbouring plains.

We then pursued our journey. I found my companion a jolly
honest plain fellow. I set out with a determined resolution
against *shaving*, that is to say, playing upon people; and therefore
I talked sensibly and roughly. We did very well till we passed
Old Camus, when one of the wheels of our chaise was so much
broke that it was of no use. The driver proposed that we should
mount the horses and ride to Berwick. But this I would by no
means agree to; and as my partner let me be the principal man
and take the direction of our journey, I made the chaise be dragged
on to Ayton, where we waited till the driver rode to Berwick
and brought us a chaise. Never did I pass three hours more
unhappily. We were set down in a cold ale-house in a little dirty
village. We had a beefsteak ill-dressed and had nothing to drink
but thick muddy beer. We were both out of humour so that we
could not speak. We tried to sleep but in vain. We only got a
drowsy headache. We were scorched by the fire on the one hand
and shivering with frost on the other. At last our chaise came,
and we got to Berwick about twelve at night. We had a slice of
hard dry toast, a bowl of warm negus, and went comfortable
to bed.

Tuesday 16 November.   We set off at six; breakfasted at Alnwick,
where we had with us a Captain Elliot of the East Indies, and

were hearty. Stewart and I began now to be acquainted and to talk about the Peace and voyages and ways of living. We had a safe day, and got at night to Durham.

Wednesday 17 November. We had a very good day of it, and got at night to Doncaster.

Thursday 18 November. We chatted a good deal. Stewart told me that some blacks in India were attacking their boat in order to plunder it, and that he shot two with his own hand. In the afternoon between Stamford and Stilton there was a young unruly horse in the chaise which run away with the driver, and jumping to one side of the road, we were overturned. We got a pretty severe rap. Stewart's head and my arm were somewhat hurt. However, we got up and pursued our way. During our last stages this night, which we travelled in the dark, I was a good deal afraid of robbers. A great many horrid ideas filled my mind. There is no passion so distressing as fear, which gives us great pain and makes us appear contemptible in our own eyes to the last degree. However, I affected resolution, and as each of us carried a loaded pistol in his hand, we were pretty secure. We got at night to Biggleswade.

Friday 19 November. It was very cold. Stewart was as effeminate as I. I asked him how he, who shivered if a pane of glass was broke in a post-chaise, could bear the severe hardship of a sea life. He gave me to understand that necessity made anything be endured. Indeed this is very true. For when the mind knows that it cannot help itself by struggling, it quietly and patiently submits to whatever load is laid upon it. When we came upon Highgate hill and had a view of London, I was all life and joy. I repeated Cato's soliloquy on the immortality of the soul, and my soul bounded forth to a certain prospect of happy futurity. I sung all manner of songs, and began to make one about an amorous meeting with a pretty girl, the burthen of which was as follows:

> She gave me *this*, I gave her *that*;
> And tell me, had she not tit for tat?

I gave three huzzas, and we went briskly in.

I got from Digges a list of the best houses on the road, and also a direction to a good inn at London. I therefore made the boy drive me to Mr Hayward's, at the Black Lion, Water Lane, Fleet Street. The noise, the crowd, the glare of shops and signs agreeably confused me. I was rather more wildly struck than when I first came to London. My companion could not understand my feelings. He considered London just as a place where he was to receive orders from the East India Company. We now parted, with saying that we had agreed well and been happy, and that we should keep up the acquaintance. I then had a bit of dinner, got myself shaved and cleaned, and had my landlord, a civil jolly man, to take a glass of wine with me. I was all in a flutter at having at last got to the place which I was so madly fond of, and being restrained, had formed so many wild schemes to get back to. I had recourse to philosophy, and so rendered myself calm.

I immediately went to my friend Douglas's, surgeon in Pall Mall, a kind-hearted, plain, sensible man, where I was cordially received. His wife is a good-humoured woman, and is that sort of character which is often met with in England: very lively without much wit. Her fault is speaking too much, which often tires people. He was my great adviser as to everything; and in the meantime insisted that I should have a bed in his house till I got a lodging to my mind. I agreed to come there next day. I went to Covent Garden—*Every Man in His Humour*. Woodward played Bobadil finely. He entertained me much. It was fine after the fatigues of my journey to find myself snug in a theatre, my body warm and my mind elegantly amused. I went to my inn, had some negus, and went comfortably to bed.

Saturday 20 November. I got into a hackney-coach with my baggage and drove to Douglas's. We calculated my expenses, and I found that to live would require great economy. However, I was upon honour to do my best. I strolled about all the forenoon calling for different people, but found nobody in. I went and saw a collection of wild beasts. I felt myself bold, easy, and happy. Only I had a kind of uneasiness from feeling no amazing difference between my existence now and at Edinburgh. I dined at Douglas's; sat in all the afternoon and wrote letters.

Sunday 21 November. I got up well and enjoyed my good situation. I had a handsome dining-room and bedchamber, just in Pall Mall, the finest part of the town; I was in pursuit of my commission, which I was vastly fond of; and I had money enough to live like a gentleman.

* * * * *

Sunday 12 December. I took a whim of dining at home every day last week, which I kept exactly to. The pleasure of gratifying whim is very great. It is known only by those who are whimsical. This day I was in a pleasing indolent humour. I sat at home writing till three, and then (as I am resolved to be at divine service every Sunday) I then went and heard prayers in St Margaret's Church, Westminster. I dined at home very comfortably. I really am very well situated in lodgings. My landlord is a jolly, civil man, his wife a quiet, well-behaved woman, and his sister a neat-handed, clever girl. They do everything to serve me. Mr Terrie is in a public office, so that he supplies me with paper and all materials for writing in great abundance, for nothing. Mrs Terrie gets all things that I want bought for me, and Miss sews the laced ruffles on my shirts, and does anything of that kind. They have always a good plain dinner. I have the art to be easy and chatty and yet maintain a proper distance. In short, I live very comfortably. I order any little alterations that I wish. For instance, there was no communication between my dining-room and bedchamber. I ordered a door to be struck out, which was instantly done. I ordered some large breakfast cups and a carpet to my bedchamber and a bureau to my dining-room. It is inconceivable with what attention and spirit I manage all my concerns. I sat in all this evening calm and indulgent. I had a fire in both my rooms above-stairs. I drank tea by myself for a long time. I had my feet washed with milk-warm water, I had my bed warmed, and went to sleep soft and contented.

Monday 13 December. I waited upon the Duke [of Queensberry], whom I found rather in better humour about my commission, as Mr Townshend had resigned, who was his great opposer. 'My Lord,' said I, 'commissions are certainly got by interest, and I know nobody who has better interest than your Grace.' He told me he had not seen Lord Ligonier, although he had called on him twice; but he promised to see him, and also to make application soon to the new Secretary at War, which, he agreed with me, might do good. I told his Grace that I would not relinquish the pursuit but wait for my commission if it should be two years. My youthful impatience was a little unsatisfied with the calm, diffident speech of the Duke, which, however, is in truth infinitely better than talking much and making me believe much more than is true.

This forenoon Mr Sheridan was with me. I told him that I had great difficulty to get to London. 'And how could it be otherwise,' said he, 'when you pushed the plan most opposite to your father's inclinations?' This immediately led us to talk fully on his scheme of the Temple, which I told him my father disapproved of, as my going to London at all was the thing that he could not think of. I told him that I could not study law, and being of a profession where you do no good is to a man of spirit very disagreeable. That I was determined to be in London. That I wanted to be something; and that the Guards was the only scene of real life that I ever liked. I feel a surprising change to the better on myself since I came to London. I am an independent man. I think myself as good as anybody, and I act entirely on my own principles. Formerly I was directed by others. I took every man's advice, that I regarded; I was fond to have it. I asked it. I told all my story freely. But now I keep my own counsel, I follow the dictates of my own good sense, than which I can see no better monitor, and I proceed consistently and resolutely. I now spoke to Sheridan with a manly firmness and a conscious assurance that I was in the right. He said that application (by which he meant business) was necessary to keep a young man from being hurried down the stream. I swelled with satisfaction at the thoughts of showing him how well I should conduct myself as an officer of the Guards.

Sir James Macdonald then came in to wait upon me for the first time. I liked to see him and Sheridan together. They fell a-talking on tragedy. Sheridan said he thought there was no occasion for our modern tragedies to be in verse. That indeed it was necessary among the ancients, as they were then set to music; but amongst us we do not require that. And indeed the actor studiously disguises the measure in reciting, and therefore why labour so much in vain? Sir James said that for domestic distress prose might do, but for kings and heroes an elevation of language is necessary. 'I don't know,' says Sheridan, 'if we may not have that in prose. Mr Macpherson in his translation of *Fingal* has shown us what dignity the English language is capable of.'

In his usual way he abused Garrick in tragedy, and said that he mimicked parts of all the good actors, but none entirely, and so appeared original. He said the taste of the age was terrible. That they would run to see an actor, being his first appearance, eagerly. 'Now,' said he, 'it would be laughed at to advertise a solo to be performed by such a man, being his first time of playing on the fiddle, or a portrait to be sold by such a man, being his first attempt in painting. And yet the mechanical part of acting is at least as difficult as that of any of these two arts. If,' said he, 'I was manager of a theatre, nobody should be allowed to come on under seven years of apprenticeship and being regularly taught.' He told us that he wanted Mrs Sheridan to write a prose tragedy.

After they left me, I went to Gould's. The Colonel had been debauching the night before and was in bed, but Mrs Gould insisted that I should eat a family dinner with her and the children, which I did very happily. Miss Fanny and I are now very good friends. 'I am sure,' said she, 'Sir, if I like any man, I like you.' She sat on the same chair with me after dinner, and sung and read very prettily. About six, Mr Gould came down to us. I gave him a genteel lecture on the advantage of temperance, and made him acknowledge that the pain of rioting much exceeded the pleasure. He was heavy, but I was lightsome and entertaining, and relieved him. I drank tea and sat the evening, gay and happy, just in the way I could wish.

Tuesday 14 December. It is very curious to think that I have now been in London several weeks without ever enjoying the delightful sex, although I am surrounded with numbers of free-hearted ladies of all kinds. . . . Fortune, or rather benignant Venus, has smiled upon me and favoured me so far that I have had the most delicious intrigues with women of beauty, sentiment, and spirit, perfectly suited to my romantic genius.

Indeed, in my mind, there cannot be higher felicity on earth enjoyed by man than the participation of genuine reciprocal affection with an amiable woman. There he has a full indulgence of all the delicate feelings and pleasures both of body and mind, while at the same time in this enchanting union he exults with a consciousness that he is the superior person. The dignity of his sex is kept up. . . . I am therefore walking about with a healthful stout body and a cheerful mind, in search of a woman worthy of my love, and who thinks me worthy of hers, without any interested views, which is the only sure way to find out if a woman really loves a man. If I should be a single man for the whole winter, I will be satisfied. I have had as much elegant pleasure as I could have expected would come to my share in many years.

However, I hope to be more successful. In this view, I had now called several times for a handsome actress of Covent Garden Theatre, whom I was a little acquainted with, and whom I shall distinguish in this my journal by the name of *Louisa*. This lady had been indisposed and saw no company, but today I was admitted. She was in a pleasing undress and looked very pretty. She received me with great politeness. We chatted on the common topics. We were not easy—there was a constraint upon us—we did not sit right on our chairs, and we were unwilling to look at one another. I talked to her on the advantage of having an agreeable acquaintance, and hoped I might see her now and then. She desired me to call in whenever I came that way, without ceremony. 'And pray,' said she, 'when shall I have the pleasure of your company at tea?' I fixed Thursday, and left her, very well satisfied with my first visit.

I then called on Mr Lee, who is a good, agreeable, honest man, and with whom I associate fine gay ideas of the Edinburgh Theatre in my boyish days, when I used to walk down the Canongate and think of players with a mixture of narrow-minded horror and lively-minded pleasure; and used to wonder at painted equipages and powdered ladies, and sing 'The bonny bush aboon Traquair,' and admire Mrs Bland in her chair with tassels, and flambeaux before her.

I did not find Lee at home. I then went to Love's. They were just sitting down to a piece of roast beef. I said that was a dish which I never let pass, and so sat down and took a slice of it. I was vexed at myself for doing it, even at the time. Love abused Mr Digges grossly; said he was a worse player than the lowest actor in Covent Garden. Their vulgarity and stupid malevolence (for Mrs Love also joined in the abuse) disgusted me much. I left them, determined scarcely to keep up an acquaintance with them, and in general to keep clear of the players, which indeed I do at present.

I dined at home. Whenever I don't mention my place of dining, it is to be understood that I dine at home. In my account of Mr Terrie's family, I neglected to mention Molly the maid, whose pardon I most sincerely ask, as she is such a personage as one does not meet with every day. She is indeed one of the stupidest human beings that I ever met with. She has not, as the philosophers say, the *anima rationalis* in a great degree, but she rather has a kind of instinct by which she is actuated, by which, however, she goes on very well. She is very careful and diligent, and extremely good-natured and disposed to oblige, and, as she is ugly, her head is not taken off from her business.

Wednesday 15 December.   The enemies of the people of England who would have them considered in the worst light represent them as selfish, beef-eaters, and cruel. In this view I resolved today to be a true-born Old Englishman. I went into the City to Dolly's Steak-house in Paternoster Row and swallowed my dinner by myself to fulfil the charge of selfishness; I had a large fat beefsteak to fulfil the charge of beef-eating; and I went at five o'clock to the Royal Cockpit in St James's Park and saw cock-fighting for about five hours to fulfil the charge of cruelty.

A beef-steakhouse is a most excellent place to dine at. You come in there to a warm, comfortable, large room, where a number of people are sitting at table. You take whatever place you find empty; call for what you like, which you get well and cleverly dressed. You may either chat or not as you like. Nobody minds you, and you pay very reasonably. My dinner (beef, bread and beer and waiter) was only a shilling. The waiters make a great deal of money by these pennies. Indeed, I admire the English for attending to small sums, as many smalls make a great, according to the proverb.

At five I filled my pockets with gingerbread and apples (quite the method), put on my old clothes and laced hat, laid by my watch, purse, and pocket-book, and with oaken stick in my hand sallied to the pit. I was too soon there. So I went into a low inn, sat down amongst a parcel of arrant blackguards, and drank some beer. The sentry near the house had been very civil in showing me the way. It was very cold. I bethought myself of the poor fellow, so I carried out a pint of beer myself to him. He was very thankful and drank my health cordially. He told me his name was Hobard, that he was a watch-maker but in distress for debt, and enlisted that his creditors might not touch him.

I then went to the Cockpit, which is a circular room in the middle of which the cocks fight. It is seated round with rows gradually rising. The pit and the seats are all covered with mat.

The cocks, nicely cut and armed with silver heels, are set down, and fight with amazing bitterness and resolution. Some of them were quickly dispatched. One pair fought three-quarters of an hour. The uproar and noise of betting is prodigious. A great deal of money made a very quick circulation from hand to hand. There was a number of professed gamblers there. An old cunning dog whose face I had seen at Newmarket sat by me a while. I told him I knew nothing of the matter. 'Sir,' said he, 'you have as good a chance as anybody.' He thought I would be a good subject for him. I was young-like. But he found himself balked. I was shocked to see the distraction and anxiety of the betters. I was sorry for the poor cocks. I looked round to see if any of the spectators pitied them when mangled and torn in a most cruel manner, but I could not observe the smallest relenting sign in any countenance. I was therefore not ill pleased to see them endure mental torment. Thus did I complete my true English day, and came home pretty much fatigued and pretty much confounded at the strange turn of this people.

Thursday 16 December. I called at the Duke's in the morning, but found that he was just setting out for Amesbury and could see nobody. This vexed me a little, as I was anxious to hear his success this week. I sat at home writing all the forenoon. I received a letter from McQuhae with an account of the death of his pupil, the only son and comfort of his parents. I was much shocked with it. Yet the consideration of the vanity of this life and the hopes of a better made me easy.

In the afternoon I went to Louisa's. A little black young fellow, her brother, came in. I could have wished him at the Bay of Honduras. However, I found him a good quiet obliging being who gave us no disturbance. She talked on a man's liking a woman's company, and of the injustice people treated them with in suspecting anything bad. This was a fine artful pretty speech. We talked of French manners, and how they studied to make one another happy. 'The English,' said I, 'accuse them of being false, because they misunderstand them. When a Frenchman makes warm professions of regard, he does it only to please you for the time. It is words, of course. There is no more of it. But the English, who are cold and phlegmatic in their address, take all these fine speeches in earnest, and are confounded to find them otherwise, and exclaim against the perfidious Gaul most unjustly. For when

Frenchmen put a thing home seriously and vow fidelity, they have the strictest honour. O they are the people who enjoy time; so lively, pleasant, and gay. You never hear of madness or self-murder among them. Heat of fancy evaporates in fine brisk clear vapour with them, but amongst the English often falls heavy upon the brain.'

We chatted pretty easily. We talked of love as a thing that could not be controlled by reason, as a fine passion. I could not clearly discern how she meant to behave to me. She told me that a gentleman had come to her and offered her £50, but that her brother knocked at the door and the man run out of the house without saying a word. I said I wished he had left his money. We joked much about the £50. I said I expected some night to be surprised with such an offer from some decent elderly gentle-woman. I made just a comic parody to her story. I sat till past eight. She said she hoped it would not be long before she had the pleasure of seeing me again.

This night I made no visible progress in my amour, but I in reality was doing a great deal. I was getting well acquainted with her. I was appearing an agreeable companion to her; I was informing her by my looks of my passion for her.

Friday 17 December.   I engaged in this amour just with a view of convenient pleasure but the god of pleasing anguish now seriously seized my breast. I felt the fine delirium of love. I waited on Louisa at one, found her alone, told her that her goodness in hoping to see me *soon* had brought me back! that it appeared long to me since I saw her. I was a little bashful. However, I took a good heart and talked with ease and dignity. 'I hope, Madam, you are at present a single woman.' 'Yes, Sir.' 'And your affections are not engaged?' 'They are not, Sir.' 'But this is leading me into a strange confession. I assure you, Madam, my affections are engaged.' 'Are they, Sir?' 'Yes, Madam, they are engaged to you.' (She looked soft and beautiful.) 'I hope we shall be better acquainted and like one another better.' 'Come, Sir, let us talk no more of that now.' 'No, Madam. I will not. It is like giving the book in the preface.' 'Just so, Sir, telling in the preface what should be in the middle of the book.' (I think such conversations are best written in the dialogue way.) 'Madam, I was very happy to find you. From the first time that I saw you, I admired you.' 'O, Sir.' 'I did indeed. What I like beyond everything is an agreeable female companion, where I can be at home and have tea and genteel conversation. I was quite happy to be here.' 'Sir, you are welcome here as often as you please. Every evening, if you please.' 'Madam, I am infinitely obliged to you.'

This is just what I wanted. I left her, in good spirits, and dined at Sheridan's. 'Well,' said he, 'are you going into the Guards?' 'Yes, Sir,' said I; 'the Temple scheme would not have done. It would only have been putting off time. I would not have applied. You cannot get a man to undergo the drudgery of the law who only wants to pass his life agreeably, and who thinks that my Lord Chancellor's four and twenty hours are not a bit happier than mine. Don't you think, Sir,' said I, 'that I am in the right to pursue the plan I like?' He replied, 'I won't speak to you on the subject. But I shall always be glad to see you.'

We talked of Johnson. He told me a story of him. 'I was dining,' said Johnson, 'with the Mayor of Windsor, who gave me a very hearty dinner; but, not satisfied with feeding my body, he would also feed my understanding. So, after he had spoke a great deal of clumsy nonsense, he told me that at the last Sessions he had transported three people to the Plantations. I was so provoked with the fellow's dullness and impertinence that I exclaimed, "I wish to GOD, Sir, I was the fourth." ' Nothing could more strongly express his dissatisfaction.

Mrs Sheridan told me that he was very sober, but would sit up the whole night. He left them once at two in the morning and begged to be excused for going away so soon, as he had another visit to make. I like to mark every anecdote of men of so much genius and literature.

I found out Sheridan's great cause of quarrel with him was that when Johnson heard of his getting a pension, 'What!' said he, 'has *he* got a pension? Then it is time for me to give up mine.' 'Now,' said he, 'here was the greatest ingratitude. For it was I and Wedderburn that first set the thing a-going.' This I believe was true.*

Mrs Sheridan told me that she was travelling in a stage-coach, and had sat silent for a long time while a fellow was chattering away like a magpie and thought they were all admiring his brightness. At last he simpered and said, 'An't I a most egregious

[*Johnson had in fact added, 'However, I am glad that Mr Sheridan has a pension, for he is a very good man', but this maliciously had not been reported to Sheridan.]

coxcomb?' 'Um?' cried an old deaf gentleman. Mrs Sheridan bawled into his ear, 'The gentleman, Sir, is a great coxcomb: he thinks we don't observe it, and he wants to tell us of it.' This confounded him so that he did not speak a word for a long time.

Mr Sheridan said that this age was (as Henry Fielding styled it) a trifling age. 'In the reign of Queen Anne,' said he, 'merit was encouraged. Then a Mr Prior was Ambassador, and a Mr Addison Secretary of State. Then genius was cherished by the beams of courtly favour. But in the reigns of George the First and George the Second it was a disadvantage to be clever. Dullness and corruption were the only means of preferment. I knew several people when at school whose Juvenilia were equal to those of the great men of letters in Queen Anne's time; but as true great genius is always accompanied with good sense, they soon saw that being men of literary merit was not the way to rise; and therefore they turned lawyers and physicians and other employments, while the buds of genius withered away.' I said I hoped we now lived in a better age, and that the reign of George the Third would give all due encouragement to genius. 'Yes,' said he, 'we may now expect that merit will flourish.' He observed that the bishops in particular were the great enemies of merit. That if a man could write well, they were of Captain Plume's opinion about the attorney: 'A dangerous man; discharge him, discharge him.' He said Lord Holdernesse with the greatest difficulty got Mr Mason, the author of *Elfrida*, a living of £200 a year.

Mrs Cholmondeley, wife to the Honourable and Reverend Mr Cholmondeley, came to tea. Her husband was an ensign in the Guards, and at the battle of Fontenoy fairly hid himself; for which he was disgracefully broke at the head of the Army. He turned clergyman, and being an earl's brother, has done very well. His lady is sister to the late Mrs Woffington, the famous actress. She is a pretty-looking woman, lively and entertaining, with that fine gay polish of manners which is only to be acquired in the genteelest company. Dr Chamberlaine, brother to Mrs Sheridan, a shrewd hearty man, was recollecting how long it was since he saw Mrs Cholmondeley. 'Just seven years, Sir,' said she. 'Madam,' said he, 'you mark time better than I do.' 'True, Sir,' replied Sheridan, 'but you must observe that time has not marked her.'

Sheridan found fault with Francis's translation of Horace. 'For,' said he, 'to give the literal meaning of Horace, it should be in verse. To give an idea of his manner and spirit, it should be imitation and applied to the present time, like Swift's two imitations, which are the only good ones.' I mentioned Pope's. 'He, Sir,' said he, 'has rather a gall of Juvenal than the delicate tartness of Horace.' This Chamberlaine and I opposed, and indeed justly. Sheridan said that selfishness was the great cause of unhappiness, and that whenever a person made self the centre, misery must ensue. I talked to him of Erskine's odd character. 'Such people,' said he, 'must have diseased minds.'

I really passed this afternoon very well, and with improvement as well as entertainment. I thought myself much happier than in the Kellie company, where mirth alone is the object; as if man was only formed a risible animal.

I mentioned to Sheridan how difficult it was to be acquainted with people of fashion in London: that they have a reserve and a forbidding shyness to strangers. He accounted for it thus: 'The strangers that come here are idle and unemployed; they don't know what to do, and they are anxious to get acquaintances. Whereas the genteel people, who have lived long in town, have got acquaintances enough; their time is all filled up. And till they find a man particularly worth knowing, they are very backward. But when you once get their friendship, you have them firm to you.'

I lamented to him the stiffness and formality of good company and the emptiness of their conversation. 'Why, Sir,' said he, 'the people of fashion in England are very ill educated and can make no figure; to disguise this and prevent such as have got parts and application from shining, conversation is just reduced to a system of insipidity, where you just repeat the most insignificant commonplace things in a sort of affected delicacy of tone. I remember,' said he, 'when the late Lord Shelburne had been some time in London, he told me that he was a very unhappy man. That before he left Ireland he used always to have the conversation of men of genius and letters; but that here he was always in the best company, where he heard nothing and could say nothing. "My Lord," said I, "will you come and eat a beefsteak with me, and I'll show you some good company." He accordingly came, and I had some men of genius, taste, and learning for him; and he was quite transported, and declared he had not passed a happy day before since he came to London.' This Sheridan told me.

Saturday 18 December. I should have mentioned yesterday that as I was sitting in my parlour after breakfast, Captain James Webster, newly arrived from Germany, came in. He looked healthy and spirited notwithstanding of all the severities that he had endured. I was very glad to see him.

This day I was rather too late in going to Child's, so that all the politics were over. I have therefore little or nothing from thence worth setting down. However, as I am a man who love forms, I shall always continue to present (such as it is) my Saturday's

Dialogue at Child's

1 CITIZEN. Pray, Doctor, what became of that patient of yours? Was not her skull fractured?

PHYSICIAN. Yes. To pieces. However, I got her cured.

1 CITIZEN. Good Lord.

Enter 2 CITIZEN *hastily.* I saw just now the Duke of Kingston pass this door, dressed more like a footman than a nobleman.

1 CITIZEN. Why, do you ever see a nobleman, dressed like himself, *walking*?

2 CITIZEN. He had just on a plain frock. If I had not seen the half of his star, I should not have known that it was him. But maybe you'll say a half-star is sometimes better than a whole moon. Eh? ha! ha! ha!

There was a hearty loud laugh.

I then went to Louisa's. I was really in love. I felt a warmth at my heart which glowed in my face. I attempted to be like Digges, and considered the similarity of our genius and pleasures. I acquired confidence by considering my present character in this light: a young fellow of spirit and fashion, heir to a good fortune, enjoying the pleasures of London, and now making his addresses in order to have an intrigue with that delicious subject of gallantry, an actress.

I talked on love very freely. 'Madam,' said I, 'I can never think of having a connection with women that I don't love.' 'That, Sir,' said she, 'is only having a satisfaction in common with the brutes. But when there is a union of minds, that is indeed estimable. But don't think, Sir, that I am a Platonist. I am not indeed.' (This hint gave me courage.) 'To be sure, Madam, when there is such a connection as you mention, it is the finest thing in the world. I beg you may just show me civility according as you find me deserve it.' 'Such a connection, Sir, requires time to establish it.' (I thought it honest and proper to let her know that she must not depend on me for giving her much money.) 'Madam,' said I, 'don't think too highly of me. Nor give me the respect which men of great fortune get by custom. I am here upon a very modest allowance. I am upon honour to make it serve me and I am obliged to live with great economy.' She received this very well.

At night I went to Mr Thomas Davies's shop and sat a while. I told him that I wanted much to see Johnson. 'Sir,' said he, 'if you'll dine with me on Christmas day, you shall see him. He and some more men of letters are to be with me.' I very readily accepted this invitation.

Sunday 19 December. The night before, I drank tea and sat all the evening writing in the room with my landlord and landlady. They insisted that I should eat a bit of supper. I complied. I also drank a glass of punch. I read some of Pope. I sung a song. I let myself down too much. Also, being unaccustomed to taste supper, my small alteration put me out of order. I went up to my room much disgusted. I thought myself a low being.

This morning I breakfasted with Mr Murray of Broughton, and then he and I went and waited on Lord and Lady Garlies, from whence we took Captain Keith Stewart with us and went to St John's Chapel and heard a tolerable sermon on humility. I was not so devout as I could have wished.

I then went to Macfarlane's. The ladies were indisposed. I could not see them. I had not been there nor seen one of the family all the week before. Captain Erskine is a most particular fellow. His indifference is amazing. He is vastly happy to have the company of people that he likes, yet he is not a bit troubled at their absence, nor will he take the smallest pains to be with them. I was really a little piqued that I had now been from him a week, that I had wished to see him, but that he had never once thought of me—which he told me. I must take him just in his own way. We were very cheerful and flighty. He abused the style of genteel company. We agreed in calling it *a consensual obliteration of the human faculties.*

I drank tea with Louisa. Her brother was there. I was very chatty and gay with looking at so fine a woman and thinking what delight I should have with her. She had a meeting with Mr Stede, an old gentleman late Prompter and now in the Cabinet Council of Covent Garden Theatre. So I was obliged to leave her at seven.

I can come home in the evening, put on my old clothes, nightcap, and slippers, and sit as contented as a cobbler writing my journal or letters to my friends. While I can thus entertain myself, I must be happy in solitude. Indeed, there is a great difference between solitude in the country, where you cannot help it, and in London, where you can in a moment be in the hurry and splendour of life.

Monday 20 December.   I went to Louisa's after breakfast. 'Indeed,' said I, 'it was hard upon me to leave you so soon yesterday. I am quite happy in your company.' 'Sir,' said she, 'you are very obliging. But,' said she, 'I am in bad humour this morning. There was a person who professed the greatest friendship for me; I now applied for their assistance, but was shifted. It was such a trifle that I am sure they could have granted it. So I have been railing against my fellow-creatures.' 'Nay, dear Madam, don't abuse them all on account of an individual. But pray what was this favour? Might I know?' (She blushed.) 'Why, Sir, there is a person has sent to me for a trifling debt. I sent back word that it was not convenient for me to let them have it just now, but in six weeks I should pay it.'

I was a little confounded and embarrassed here. I dreaded bringing myself into a scrape. I did not know what she might call a trifling sum. I half-resolved to say no more. However, I thought that she might now be trying my generosity and regard for her, and truly this was the real test. I thought I would see if it was in my power to assist her.

'Pray, Madam, what was the sum?' 'Only two guineas, Sir.' Amazed and pleased, I pulled out my purse. 'Madam,' said I, 'if I can do you any service, you may command me. Two guineas is at present all that I have, but a trifle more. There they are for you. I told you that I had very little, but yet I hope to live. Let us just be honest with one another. Tell me when you are in any little distress, and I will tell you what I can do.' She took the guineas. 'Sir, I am infinitely obliged to you. As soon as it is in my power, I shall return them. Indeed I could not have expected this from you.' Her gratitude warmed my heart. 'Madam!

though I have little, yet as far as ten guineas, you may apply to me. I would live upon nothing to serve one that I regarded.'

I did not well know what to think of this scene. Sometimes I thought it artifice, and that I was taken in. And then again, I viewed it just as a circumstance that might very easily happen. Her mentioning returning the money looked well. My naming the sum of ten guineas was rash; however . . . ten guineas was but a moderate expense for women during the winter.

I had all along treated her with a distant politeness. On Saturday I just kissed her hand. She now sung to me. I got up in raptures and kissed her with great warmth. She received this very genteelly. I had a delicacy in presuming too far, lest it should look like demanding goods for my money. I resumed the subject of love and gallantry. She said, 'I pay no regard to the opinion in the world so far as contradicts my own sentiments.' 'No, Madam, we are not to mind the arbitrary rules imposed by the multitude.' 'Yet, Sir, there is a decency to be kept with the public. And I must do so, whose bread depends upon them.' 'Certainly, Madam. But when may I wait upon you? Tomorrow evening?' 'Sir, I am obliged to be all day with a lady who is not well.' 'Then next day, Madam.' 'What? to drink a dish of tea, Sir?' 'No, no, not to drink a dish of tea.' (Here I looked sheepish.) 'What time may I wait upon you?' 'Whenever you please, Sir.' I kissed her again, and went away highly pleased with the thoughts of the affair being settled.

I dined at Macfarlane's. We were very hearty. I indulged in it much. Erskine and I walked down the Haymarket together, throwing out sallies and laughing aloud. 'Erskine,' said I, 'don't I make your existence pass more cleverly than anybody?' 'Yes. You extract more out of me, you are more chemical to me, than anybody.' We drank tea at Dempster's.

I went and sat a while with Captain Webster. He told me that the fatigues of a German campaign are almost incredible. That he was fourteen nights running without being under cover, and often had scarcely any victuals. He said he never once repented his being a soldier, although he cursed the sad fatigues. 'Men,' said he, 'are in that way rendered desperate; and I have wished for an action, either to get out of the world altogether or to get a little rest after it.' We talked on a variety of old stories. He is a lively young fellow, and has humour. We were very merry. He returned me many thanks for my company and said it revived him.

Tuesday 21 December.   I had resolved not to dine with my land-lord, nor to see them much this week, in order to recover my proper dignity and distance. Another very good reason now glared me strong in the face. By my letting Louisa have two guineas, I had only thirteen shillings left; and my term of payment, as I have £25 every six weeks, was not till the 7 of January. I therefore could not afford a shilling, nor near so much, for dinner. So that I was put to my shifts, as I would not be indebted for dinner nor go and ask my allowance before it was due. I sat in till between four and five. I then went to Holborn, to a cheese-monger's, and bought a piece of 3 lb. 10 oz., which cost me 14½d. I eat part of it in the shop, with a halfpenny roll, two of which I had bought at a baker's. I then carried home my provision, and eat some more cheese with the other roll, and a half pennyworth of apples by way of relish, and took a drink of water. I recollected that I had left a guinea of security at Noble's circulating library. I went and told him that he should put confidence in me, so got it back. This was a most welcome guest to my pocket and communicated spirit to my heart. But, alas, of short duration was this state of opulence. I was reminded by Miss Terrie of a pair of lace ruffles that I had bespoke, which came to 16s. 'Very well,' said I, and paid them. There was the genteel determined spirit. I comforted myself by thinking that I suffered in the service of my Mistress; and I was romantically amused to think that I was now obliged to my wits, and living on the profit of my works, having got just 13s. by my *Cub.*

I should have mentioned that on Monday Captain Douglas of Kelhead and Captain Maxwell of Dalswinton breakfasted with me.

This evening I had a little adventure which took away the twenty-sixth part of my little stock. I was passing by Whitehall when a little boy came and told a girl who sold gingerbread nuts that he had just given her sixpence instead of a farthing. She denied this. Upon which the poor boy cried and lamented most bitterly. I thought myself bound to interfere in the affair. The boy affirmed the charge with the open keen look of conscious innocence, while the young jade denied it with the colour of countenance and bitterness of expression that betrayed guilt. But what could be done? There was no proof. At last I put it to this test: 'Will you say, Devil take you, if you got his sixpence?' This imprecation the little gipsy roared out twice most fervently.

Therefore she got off. No jury in any court could have brought her in guilty. There was now a good many people assembled about us. The boy was in very great distress. I asked him if the sixpence was his own. He said it was his mother's. I conceived the misery of his situation when he got home. 'There, Sir,' said I, 'is the sixpence to you. Go home and be easy.' I then walked on much satisfied with myself. Such a little incident as this might be laughed at as trifling. But I cannot help thinking it amusing, and valuing it as a specimen of my own tenderness of disposition and willingness to relieve my fellow-creatures.

Wednesday 22 December. I stood and chatted a while with the sentries before Buckingham House. One of them, an old fellow, said he was in all the last war. 'At the battle of Dettingen,' said he, 'I saw our cannon make a line through the French army as broad as that' (pointing to the Mall), 'which was filled up in as short time as I'm telling you it.' They asked me for a pint of beer, which I gave them. I talked on the sad mischief of war and on the frequency of poverty. 'Why, Sir,' said he, 'GOD made all right at first when he made mankind. ('I believe,' said the other, 'he made but few of them.') But, Sir, if GOD was to make the world today, it would be crooked again tomorrow. But the time will come when we shall all be rich enough. To be sure, salvation is promised to those that die in the field.' I have great pleasure in conversing with the lower part of mankind, who have very curious ideas.

This forenoon I went to Louisa's in full expectation of consummate bliss. I was in a strange flutter of feeling. I was ravished at the prospect of joy, and yet I had such an anxiety upon me that I was afraid that my powers would be enervated. I almost wished to be free of this assignation. I entered her apartment in a sort of confusion. She was elegantly dressed in the morning fashion, and looked delightfully well. I felt the tormenting anxiety of serious love. I sat down and I talked with the distance of a new acquaintance and not with the ease and ardour of a lover, or rather a gallant. I talked of her lodgings being neat, opened the door of her bedchamber, looked into it. Then sat down by her in a most melancholy plight. I would have given a good deal to be out of the room.

We talked of religion. Said she, 'People who deny that, show a want of sense.' 'For my own part, Madam, I look upon the adoration of the Supreme Being as one of the greatest enjoyments we have. I would not choose to get rid of my religious notions. I have read books that staggered me. But I was glad to find myself regain my former opinions.' 'Nay, Sir, what do you think of the Scriptures having stood the test of ages?' 'Are you a Roman Catholic, Madam?' 'No, Sir. Though I like some parts of their religion, in particular, confession; not that I think the priest can remit sins, but because the notion that we are to confess to a decent clergyman may make us cautious what we do.' 'Madam,' said I, 'I would ask you to do nothing that you should be sorry to confess. Indeed I have a great deal of principle in matters of gallantry, and never yet led any woman to do what might after- wards make her uneasy. If she thinks it wrong, I never insist.' She asked me some questions about my intrigues, which I nicely eluded.

I then sat near her and began to talk softly, but finding myself quite dejected with love, I really cried out and told her that I was miserable; and as I was stupid, would go away. I rose, but saluting her with warmth, my powers were excited, I felt myself vigorous. I sat down again. I beseeched her, 'You know, Madam, you said you was not a Platonist. I beg it of you to be so kind. You said you are above the finesse of your sex.' (Be sure always to make a woman better than her sex.) 'I adore you.' 'Nay, dear Sir' (I pressing her to me and kissing her now and then) 'pray be quiet. Such a thing requires time to consider of.' 'Madam, I own this would be necessary for any man but me. But you must take my character from myself. I am very good-tempered, very honest, and have little money. I should have some reward for my parti- cular honesty.' 'But, Sir, give me time to recollect myself.' 'Well then, Madam, when shall I see you?' 'On Friday, Sir.' 'A thousand thanks.' I left her and came home and took my bread and cheese with great contentment, and then went and chatted a while with Webster.

I had not been at Lord Eglinton's for ten days. Last night I received a card from him: 'Lord Eglinton presents his compli- ments to Mr Boswell, and returns him a great many thanks for being so good as to call on him so often. He is sorry he happened to be always out when Mr Boswell called.'

This he intended as a sharp reproof. However, as Lord North- umberland had called for me, I thought Lord Eglinton might do so, as I was quite independent of him. The card was not written with his own hand, which I was not pleased at. I am the easiest fellow in the world to those who behave well to me. But if a man has treated me with the least slight, I will keep him to every punctilio. I sent him for answer: 'Mr Boswell presents his compliments to Lord Eglinton; hopes he will excuse his writing this card with his own hand; he has not a secretary. Mr Boswell has paid his respects to Lord Eglinton several times. He lodges at Mr Terrie's in Downing Street.'

This had a proper effect, for today he called when I was abroad, which satisfied me much.

I sat this evening a while with Webster. He entertained me and raised my spirits with military conversation. Yet he sunk them a little; as he brought into my mind some dreary Tolbooth Kirk ideas, than which nothing has given me more gloomy feelings. I shall never forget the dismal hours of apprehension that I have endured in my youth from narrow notions of religion while my tender mind was lacerated with infernal horror. I am surprised how I have got rid of these notions so entirely. Thank GOD, my mind is now clear and elevated. I am serene and happy. I can look up to my Creator with adoration and hope.

Thursday 23 December.   I should have mentioned some days ago that Erskine and I took a walk in St James's Park, on a fine, sunshine forenoon. I told him that if the Guards could not be got for me, I would just take a cornetcy of Dragoons. 'I beseech you,' said he, 'never think of that. You would grow melancholy. You would destroy yourself. If you was sent by yourself to country quarters, I would not trust you with a basin of cold water to wash your hands, nor with the most awkward imitation of a penknife.'

I had this day a walk there with Sheridan. Said he, 'Our present plan of education is very bad. A young man is taught for a number of years a variety of things which, when he comes into the world, he finds of no manner of use. There is not one thing taught for the conduct of real life. The mind is ploughed and harrowed, but there is no seed sown. By cultivation the soil is made rich, and so when a young man comes into the world, whatever happens to be sown grows up in great luxuriance. A strong proof that the minds of the people of England are not formed is their instability. In Oliver Cromwell's time they were all precise, canting creatures. And no sooner did Charles the Second come over than they turned gay rakes and libertines. In James the First's time, the Duke of

Buckingham, who wanted to rival Cardinal Richelieu in every-thing, brought about a Parliamentary inquiry into the state of education, that he might do as much in that way as the great Minister of France; but by the Duke's death this did not take place, at least was not carried through. Without such a scheme, we cannot hope for a proper plan of education. But this, I have reason to believe, will be one of the first objects after the Peace. My plan would be that young people should be perfectly qualified to be good citizens in the first place, and that there should be particular opportunities of instruction for every particular way of life. There is one rank for which there is no plan of education, and that is country gentlemen. Surely, this is of great importance: that the landed interest should be well instructed.' 'Mr Sheridan,' said I, 'I have thought a good deal upon education. I see so many difficulties that I despair of a good method. I take this state of being to be a jest; that it is not intended that we should do much here to the purpose; and therefore we must just go through it the best way we can.' 'Nay, Sir,' said he, 'we can do something to the purpose.' Indeed it is more agreeable to think of doing something than to consider ourselves as nothing at all.

I eat my cold repast today heartily. I have great spirits. I see how little a man can live upon. I find that Fortune cannot get the better of me. I never can come lower than to live on bread and cheese.

Friday 24 December. I waited on Louisa. Says she, 'I have been very unhappy since you was here. I have been thinking of what I said to you. I find that such a connection would make me miser-able.' 'I hope, Madam, I am not disagreeable to you.' 'No Sir, you are not. If it was the first duke in England I spoke to, I should just say the same thing.' 'But pray, Madam, what is your objec-tion?' 'Really Sir, I have many disagreeable apprehensions. It may be known. Circumstances might be very troublesome. I beg it of you, Sir, consider of it. Your own good sense will agree with me. Instead of visiting me as you do now, you would find a discontented, unhappy creature.' I was quite confused. I did not know what to say. At last I agreed to think of it and see her on Sunday. I came home and dined in dejection. Yet I mustered up vivacity, and away I went in full dress to Northum-berland House. There was spirit, to lay out a couple of shillings and be a man of fashion in my situation. There was true economy.

Saturday 25 December. The night before I did not rest well. I was really violently in love with Louisa. I thought she did not care for me. I thought that if I did not gain her affections, I would appear despicable to myself. This day I was in a better frame, being Christmas day, which has always inspired me with most agreeable feelings. I went to St Paul's Church and in that magnificent temple fervently adored the God of goodness and mercy, and heard a sermon by the Bishop of Oxford on the publishing of glad tidings of great joy. I then went to Child's, where little was passing. However, here goes the form of a

Dialogue at Child's

1 CITIZEN. Why, here is the bill of mortality. Is it right, Doctor?
PHYSICIAN. Why, I don't know.
1 CITIZEN. I'm sure it is not. Sixteen only died of cholics! I dare say you killed as many yourself.
2 CITIZEN. Ay and hanged but three! O Lord, ha! ha! ha!

I then sat a while at Coutts's, and then at Macfarlane's, and then went to Davies's. Johnson was gone to Oxford. I was introduced to Mr Dodsley, a good, jolly, decent, conversable man, and Mr Goldsmith, a curious, odd, pedantic fellow with some genius. It was quite a literary dinner. I had seen no warm victuals for four days, and therefore played a very bold knife and fork. It is inconceivable how hearty I eat and how comfortable I felt myself after it. We talked entirely in the way of Geniuses.

We talked of poetry. Said GOLDSMITH, 'The miscellaneous poetry of this age is nothing like that of the last; it is very poor. Why there, now, Mr Dodsley, is your *Collection.*' DODSLEY: 'I think that equal to those made by Dryden and Pope.' GOLDSMITH: 'To consider them, Sir, as villages, yours may be as good; but let us compare house with house, you can produce me no edifices equal to the *Ode on St Cecilia's Day, Absalom and Achitophel*, or *The Rape of the Lock.*' DODSLEY: 'We have poems in a different way. There is nothing of the kind in the last age superior to *The Spleen.*' BOSWELL: 'And what do you think of Gray's odes? Are not they noble?' GOLDSMITH: 'Ah, the rumbling thunder! I remember a friend of mine was very fond of Gray. "Yes," said I, "he is very fine indeed: as thus—

> Mark the white and mark the red,
> Mark the blue and mark the green;
> Mark the colours ere they fade,
> Darting thro' the welkin sheen."

"O, yes," said he, "great, great!" "True, Sir," said I, "but I have made the lines this moment." ' BOSWELL: 'Well, I admire Gray prodigiously. I have read his odes till I was almost mad.' GOLDSMITH: 'They are terribly obscure. We must be historians and learned men before we can understand them.' DAVIES: 'And why not? He is not writing to porters or carmen. He is writing to men of knowledge.' GOLDSMITH: 'Have you seen *Love in a Village?*' BOSWELL: 'I have. I think it a good, pleasing thing.' GOLDSMITH: 'I am afraid we will have no good plays now. The taste of the audience is spoiled by the pantomime of Shakespeare. The wonderful changes and shiftings.' DAVIES: 'Nay, but you will allow that Shakespeare has great merit?' GOLDSMITH: 'No, I know Shakespeare very well.' (Here I said nothing, but thought him a most impudent puppy.) BOSWELL: 'What do you think of Johnson?' GOLDSMITH: 'He has exceeding great merit. His *Rambler* is a noble work.' BOSWELL: 'His *Idler* too is very pretty. It is a lighter performance; and he has thrown off the classical fetters very much.' DAVIES: 'He is a most entertaining companion. And how can it be otherwise, when he has so much imagination, has read so much, and digested it so well?'

We had many more topics which I don't remember. I was very well. I then went to Macfarlane's. We were very merry. Erskine and I had some bread and wine and talked for near two hours. He told me that he was kept as a blackguard when he was a boy, then went to sea, and then came into the Army. And that he wondered how he had been turned out a tolerable being.

Sunday 26 December. I went to Whitehall Chapel and heard service. I took a whim to go through all the churches and chapels in London, taking one each Sunday.

At one I went to Louisa's. I told her my passion in the warmest terms. I told her that my happiness absolutely depended upon her. She said it was running the greatest risk. 'Then,' said I 'Madam, you will show the greatest generosity to a most sincere lover.' She said that we should take time to consider of it, and that then we could better determine how to act. We agreed that the time should be a week, and that if I remained of the same opinion, she would then make me blessed. There is no telling how easy it made my mind to be convinced that she did not despise me, but on the contrary had a tender heart and wished to make me easy and happy.

I this day received a letter from the Duke of Queensberry, in answer to one that I had wrote him, telling me that a commission in the Guards was a fruitless pursuit, and advising me to take to a civil rather than a military life. I was quite stupefied and enraged at this. I imagined my father was at the bottom of it. I had multitudes of wild schemes. I thought of enlisting for five years as a soldier in India, of being a private man either in the Horse or Foot Guards, &c. At last good sense prevailed, and I resolved to be cheerful and to wait and to ask it of Lady Northumberland. At night I sat at Macfarlane's pretty well.

The decision to take to a civil rather than a military life stayed in abeyance until Wednesday 8 June 1763, when Boswell received 'a most sensible and indulgent letter' from his father, Lord Auchinleck. While prepared to allow his son to follow any profession of his choice, Lord Auchinleck, himself a judge, thought little of the Army scheme and would far sooner encourage him to take up law. Boswell had been disappointed in his hopes of help from the aristocracy and now thought he would have little chance of Army preferment. Civilian life looked smooth and easy in comparison. A legal career would please his father who was, he said, one of the best men in the world, despite the narrowness of his notions. After some two years of energetic travel on the Continent, Boswell was admitted to the Faculty of Advocates on July 26, 1766, and practised law in Edinburgh for seventeen years.

For Louisa Lewis's exit, and Mr Samuel Johnson's entrance, see the Foreword, pages 10 and 11. Boswell's Journal of the Tour to the Hebrides *was published in 1786—Johnson had died in December, 1784—and the great* Life *appeared five years later.*

4

The Carlyles
Consider
The Past

THOMAS CARLYLE and
JANE WELSH CARLYLE

1   *THOMAS CARLYLE reviews John Wilson Croker's edition of*
Boswell's Life of Johnson: 1831

... We have next a word to say of James Boswell. Boswell has
already been much commented upon; but rather in the way of
censure and vituperation than of true recognition. He was a man
that brought himself much before the world; confessed that he
eagerly coveted fame, or if that were not possible, notoriety; of
which latter as he gained far more than seemed his due, the
public were incited, not only by their natural love of scandal,
but by a special ground of envy, to say whatever ill of him could
be said. Out of the fifteen millions that then lived, and had bed
and board, in the British Islands, this man has provided us a
greater *pleasure* than any other individual, at whose cost we now
enjoy ourselves; perhaps has done us a greater *service* than can be
specially attributed to more than two or three: yet, ungrateful
that we are, no written or spoken eulogy of James Boswell
anywhere exists; his recompense in solid pudding (so far as
copyright went) was not excessive; and as for the empty praise,
it has altogether been denied him. Men are unwiser than children;
they do *not* know the hand that feeds them.

Boswell was a person whose mean or bad qualities lay open to
the general eye; visible, palpable to the dullest. His good qualities,

again, belonged not to the Time he lived in; were far from common then; indeed, in such a degree, were almost unexampled; not recognizable therefore by every one; nay, apt even (so strange had they grown) to be confounded with the very vices they lay contiguous to, and had sprung out of. That he was a wine-bibber and gross-liver; gluttonously fond of whatever would yield him a little solacement, were it only of a stomachic character, is undeniable enough. That he was vain, heedless, a babbler; had much of the sycophant, alternating with the braggadocio, curiously spiced too with an all-pervading dash of the coxcomb; that he gloried much when the Tailor, by a court-suit, had made a new man of him; that he appeared at the Shakespeare Jubilee with a riband, imprinted *Corsica Boswell*, round his hat; and in short, if you will, lived no day of his life without doing and saying more than one pretentious ineptitude: all this unhappily is evident as the sun at noon. The very look of Boswell seems to have signified so much. In that cocked nose, cocked partly in triumph over his weaker fellow-creatures, partly to snuff up the smell of coming pleasure, and scent it from afar; in those bag-cheeks, hanging like half-filled wine-skins, still able to contain more; in that coarsely-protruded shelf-mouth, that fat dewlapped chin; in all this, who sees not sensuality, pretension, boisterous imbecility enough; much that could not have been ornamental in the temper of a great man's overfed great man (what the Scotch name *flunky*), though it had been more natural there? The under part of Boswell's face is of a low, almost brutish character.

Unfortunately, on the other hand, what great and genuine good lay in him was nowise so self-evident. That Boswell was a hunter after spiritual Notabilities, that he loved such, and longed, and even crept and crawled to be near them; that he first (in old Touchwood Auchinleck's phraseology) 'took on with Paoli'; and then being off with 'the Corsican landlouper', took on with a schoolmaster, 'ane that keeped a schule and ca'd it an academy': that he did all this, and could not help doing it, we account a very singular merit. The man, once for all, had an 'open sense', an open, loving heart, which so few have: where Excellence existed, he was compelled to acknowledge it; was drawn towards it, and (let the old sulphur-brand of a Laird say what he liked) *could not but* walk with it—if not as superior, if not as equal, then as inferior and lackey, better so than not at all. If we reflect now that his love of Excellence had not only such an evil *nature* to triumph over; but also what an *education* and social position withstood it and weighed it down, its innate strength, victorious over all these things, may astonish us. Consider what an inward impulse there must have been, how many mountains of impediment hurled aside, before the Scottish Laird could, as humble servant, embrace the knees (the bosom was not permitted him) of the English Dominie! Your Scottish Laird, says an English naturalist of these days, may be defined as the hungriest and vainest of all bipeds yet known. Boswell too was a Tory; of quite peculiarly feudal, genealogical, pragmatical temper; had been nurtured in an atmosphere of Heraldry, at the feet of a very Gamaliel in that kind; within bare walls, adorned only with pedigrees, amid serving-men in threadbare livery; all things teaching him, from birth upwards, to remember that a Laird was a Laird. Perhaps there was a special vanity in his very blood: old Auchinleck had, if not the gay, tail-spreading, peacock vanity of his son, no little of the slow-stalking, contentious, hissing vanity of the gander; a still more fatal species.

And now behold the worthy Bozzy, so prepossessed and held back by nature and by art, fly nevertheless like iron to its magnet, whither his better genius called! You may surround the iron and the magnet with what enclosures and encumbrances you please— with wood, with rubbish, with brass: it matters not, the two feel each other, they struggle restlessly towards each other, they *will* be together. The iron may be a Scottish squirelet, full of gulosity and 'gigmanity'; the magnet an English plebeian, and moving rag-and-dust mountain, coarse, proud, irascible, imperious: nevertheless, behold how they embrace, and inseparably cleave to one another! It is one of the strangest phenomena of the past century, that at a time when the old reverent feeling of Discipleship (such as brought men from far countries, with rich gifts, and prostrate soul, to the feet of the Prophets) had passed utterly away from men's practical experience, and was no longer surmised to exist (as it does), perennial, indestructible, in man's inmost heart— James Boswell should have been the individual, of all others, pre-destined to recall it, in such singular guise, to the wondering, and, for a long while, laughing and unrecognizing world. It has been commonly said, The man's vulgar vanity was all that attached him to Johnson; he delighted to be seen near him, to be thought connected with him. Now let it be at once granted that

no consideration springing out of vulgar vanity could well be
absent from the mind of James Boswell, in this his intercourse
with Johnson, or in any considerable transaction of his life. At the
same time, ask yourself: Whether such vanity, and nothing else,
actuated him therein; whether this was the true essence and
moving principle of the phenomenon, or not rather its outward
vesture, and the accidental environment (and defacement) in
which it came to light? The man was, by nature and habit, vain;
a sycophant-coxcomb, be it granted: but had there been nothing
more than vanity in him, was Samuel Johnson the man of men
to whom he must attach himself? At the date when Johnson was a
poor rusty-coated 'scholar', dwelling in Temple-lane, and indeed
throughout their whole intercourse afterwards, were there not
chancellors and prime ministers enough; graceful gentlemen, the
glass of fashion; honour-giving noblemen; dinner-giving rich
men; renowned fire-eaters, swordsmen, gownsmen; Quacks and
Realities of all hues—any one of whom bulked much larger in
the world's eye than Johnson ever did? To any one of whom, by
half that submissiveness and assiduity, our Bozzy might have
recommended himself; and sat there, the envy of surrounding
lickspittles; pocketing now solid emolument, swallowing now
well-cooked viands and wines of rich vintage; in each case, also,
shone on by some glittering reflex of Renown or Notoriety, so
as to be the observed of innumerable observers. To no one of
whom, however, though otherwise a most diligent solicitor and
purveyor, did he so attach himself: such vulgar courtierships
were his paid drudgery, or leisure amusement; the worship of
Johnson was his grand, ideal, voluntary business. Does not the
frothy-hearted, yet enthusiastic man, doffing his Advocate's-wig,
regularly take post, and hurry up to London, for the sake of his
Sage chiefly; as to a Feast of Tabernacles, the Sabbath of his
whole year? The plate-licker and wine-bibber dives into Bolt
Court, to sip muddy coffee with a cynical old man, and a sour-
tempered blind old woman (feeling the cups, whether they are
full, with her finger); and patiently endures contradictions
without end; too happy so he may but be allowed to listen and
live. Nay, it does not appear that vulgar vanity could ever have
been much flattered by Boswell's relation to Johnson. His devout
Discipleship seemed nothing more than a mean Spanielship, in
the general eye. His mighty 'constellation', or sun, round whom
he, as satellite, observantly gyrated, was, for the mass of men,

but a huge ill-snuffed tallow-light, and he a weak night-moth, circling foolishly, dangerously about it, not knowing what he wanted. Doubtless the man was laughed at, and often heard himself laughed at for his Johnsonism. To be envied is the grand and sole aim of vulgar vanity; to be filled with good things is that of sensuality: for Johnson perhaps no man living *envied* poor Bozzy: and of good things (except himself paid for them) there was no vestige in that acquaintanceship. Had nothing other or better than vanity and sensuality been there, Johnson and Boswell had never come together, or had soon and finally separated again.

In fact, the so copious terrestrial dross that welters chaotically, as the outer sphere of this man's character, does but render for us more remarkable, more touching, the celestial spark of goodness, of light, and Reverence for Wisdom, which dwelt in the interior, and could struggle through such encumbrances, and in some degree illuminate and beautify them. There is much lying yet undeveloped in the love of Boswell for Johnson.

... As for the Book itself, questionless the universal favour entertained for it is well merited. In worth as a Book we have rated it beyond any other product of the eighteenth century: all Johnson's own Writings, laborious and in their kind genuine above most, stand on a quite inferior level to it; already, indeed, they are becoming obsolete for this generation; and for some future generation may be valuable chiefly as Prolegomena and expository Scholia to this *Johnsoniad* of Boswell. Which of us remembers, as one of the sunny spots of his existence, the day when he opened these airy volumes, fascinating him by a true natural magic! It was as if the curtains of the past were drawn aside, and we looked mysteriously into a kindred country, where dwelt our Fathers; inexpressibly dear to us, but which had seemed forever hidden from our eyes. For the dead Night had engulfed it; all was gone, vanished as if it had not been. Nevertheless, wondrously given back to us, there once more it lay; all bright, lucid, blooming; a little island of Creation amid the circumambient Void. There it still lies; like a thing stationary, imperishable, over which changeful Time were now accumulating itself in vain, and could not, any longer, harm it, or hide it.

2   *JANE WELSH CARLYLE describes her return to her old home,*
Haddington, East Lothian: 1849

From Morpeth to Haddington is a journey of only four hours;
—rapidest travelling to Scotland now, and no home there any
more! The first locality I recognized was the Peer Bridge; I had
been there once before, a little child, in a post-chaise with my
father; he had held his arm round me while I looked down the
ravine. It was my first sight of the picturesque, that. I recognized
the place even in passing it at railway speed, after all these long,
long years.

At the Dunbar station an old lady in widow's dress, and a
young one, her daughter, got into the carriage, which I had had
so far all to myself; a man in yeomanry uniform waiting to see
them off. 'Ye'll maybe come and see us the morn's nicht?' said
the younger lady from the carriage. 'What for did ye no come to
the ball?' answered the yeoman, with a look 'to split a pitcher'.
The young lady tchicked-tchicked, and looked deprecatingly,
and tried again and again to enchain conversation; but to everything she said came the same answer—'What for did ye no come
to the ball?' The poor young lady then tried holding her tongue;
her lover (only her lover would have used her so brutally) did
the same; but rested his chin on the carriage window to scowl at
her with more convenience. The interest was rising; but one
could see who of them would speak first. 'Oh!' broke out the
young lady, 'I'm just mourning.' 'What for?' 'Oh, just that ball!'
'What for then did ye no come?' growled the repeating decimal;
'I waited an oor for ye!' and he got his upper lip over the strap
of his cap and champed it—like a horse! Squeal went the engine;
we were off; the young lady 'just mourned' for a minute or two,
then fell to talking with her mother. Before the ladies got out
at Drem I had identified the pale, old, shrivelled widow with a
buxom, bright-eyed, rosy Mrs Frank Sheriff of my time. The
daughter had not only grown up but got herself born in the
interval. What chiefly struck me, however—indeed confounded
me—was to be stared at by Mrs Sheriff as a stranger! I began to
think my precautions for keeping *incognita* in my native place
might turn out to have been superfluous. . . .

5

... A few minutes more and I was at the Haddington station, where I looked out timidly, then more boldly, as my senses took in the utter strangeness of the scene; and luckily I had 'the cares of luggage' to keep down sentiment for the moment. No vehicle was in waiting but a little dusty omnibus, licensed to carry any number, it seemed; for, on remarking there was no seat for me, I was told by all the insides in a breath, 'Never heed! come in! that makes no difference!' And so I was trundled to the 'George Inn', where a landlord and waiter, both strangers to me, and looking half-asleep, showed me to the best room on the first floor, a large, old-fashioned, three-windowed room, looking out on Fore Street, and, without having spoken one word, shut the door on me, and there I was at the end of it! Actually in the 'George Inn', Haddington, alone, amidst the silence of death!

I sat down quite composedly at a window, and looked up the street towards our old house. It was the same street, the same houses: but so silent, dead, petrified! It looked the old place just as I had seen it at Chelsea in my dreams, only more dream-like! I rang my bell, and told the silent landlord to bring tea and take order about my bedroom. The tea swallowed down, I notified my wish to view 'the old church there', and the keeper of the keys was immediately fetched me. In my part of Stranger in search of the Picturesque. I let myself be shown the way which I knew every inch of, shown 'the school-house' where myself had been Dux, 'the play-ground', 'the boolin' green', and so on to the church-gate; which so soon as my guide had unlocked for me, I told him that I needed him no further.

The churchyard had become very full of graves; within the ruin were two new smartly got-up tombs. *His*, my father's, looked old, old; was surrounded by nettles: the inscription all over moss, except two lines which had been quite recently cleaned—by whom? Who had been there before me, still caring for his tomb after twenty-nine years? The old ruin knew, and could not tell me. That place felt the very centre of eternal silence—silence and sadness world without end! When I returned, the sexton, or whatever he was, asked, 'Would I not walk through the church?' I said 'Yes', and he led the way, but without playing the cicerone any more; he had become pretty sure there was no need. Our pew looked to have never been new-lined since we occupied it; the green cloth was become all but white from age! I looked at it in the dim twilight till I almost fancied I saw my beautiful mother in her old corner, and myself, a bright-looking girl, in the other! It was time to 'come out of that!' Meaning to return to the churchyard next morning, to clear the moss from the inscription, I asked my conductor where he lived—with his key. 'Next door to the house that was Dr Welsh's,' he answered, with a sharp glance at my face; then added gently, 'Excuse me, me'm, for mentioning that, but the minute I set eyes on ye at the "George", I jaloosed it was her we all looked after whenever she went up or down.' 'You won't tell of me?' I said, crying, like a child caught stealing apples; and gave him half-a-crown to keep my secret, and open the gate for me at eight next morning. Then, turning up the waterside by myself, I made the circuit of The Haugh, Dodds's Gardens and Babbie's Butts, the customary evening walk in my teens; and except that it was perfectly solitary, the whole thing looked exactly as I left it twenty-three years back; the very puddles made by the last rain I felt to have stepped over before. Leaving the lanes, I now went boldly through the streets, the thick black veil, put on for the occasion, thrown back; I was getting up confidence that I might have ridden like the Lady Godiva through Haddington, with impunity, so far as recognition went. I looked through the sparred door of our old coach-house, which seemed to be vacant; the house itself I left over till morning, when its occupants should be asleep. Passing a cooper's shop, which I had once had the run of, I stept in and bought two little quaighs; then in the character of travelling Englishwoman, suddenly seized with an unaccountable passion for wooden dishes, I questioned the cooper as to the past and present of his town. He was the very man for me, being ready to talk the tongue small in his head about his town's-folks—men, women, and children of them. He told me, amongst other interesting things, 'Doctor Welsh's death was the sorest loss ever came to the place', that myself 'went away into England and—died there!' adding a handsome enough tribute to my memory. 'Yes! Miss Welsh! he remembered her famously, used to think her the tastiest young lady in the whole place; but she was very—not just to call proud—very reserved in her company.' In leaving this man I felt more than ever like my own ghost; if I had been walking after my death and burial, there could not, I think, have been any material difference in my speculations.

My next visit was to the front gate of Sunny Bank, where I stood some minutes, looking up at the beautifully quiet house.

How would my old godmother and the others have looked, I wondered, had they known who was there so near them? I longed to go in and kiss them once more, but positively dared not; I felt that their demonstrations of affection would break me down into a torrent of tears, which there was no time for; so I contented myself with kissing the gate (!) and returned to my inn, it being now near dark.

On my re-entry I rang for candles, and for a glass of sherry and hot water; my feet had been wetted amongst the long grass of the churchyard, and I felt to be taking cold; so I made myself negus as an antidote, and they say I am not a practical woman!

I slept in the first instance, for I was 'a-weary, a-weary', body and soul of me! But, alas! the only noise I was to hear in Haddington transpired exactly at the wrong moment; before I had slept one hour I was awoke by—an explosion of cats! The rest of the night I spent betwixt sleeping and waking. At half after five I put my clothes on, and began the business of the day. Soon after six I was haunting our old house, while the present occupants still slept. I found the garden door locked, and iron stanchions —my heavens!—on the porch and cellar windows, 'significative of much'! For the rest, there was a general need of paint and whitewash; in fact, the whole premises had a bedimmed, melancholy look as of having 'seen better days'.

It was difficult for me to realize to myself that the people inside were only asleep, and not dead—dead since many years. Ah! one breathed freer in the churchyard, with the bright morning sunshine streaming down on it, than near that (so-called) habitation of the living! I went straight from one to the other. The gate was still locked, for I was an hour before my time: so I made a dash at the wall, some seven feet high I should think, and dropt safe on the inside—a feat I should never have imagined to try in my actual phase, not even with a mad bull at my heels, if I had not trained myself to it at a more elastic age.

When I had scraped the moss out of the inscription as well as I could with the only thing in my dressing case at all suited to the purpose, namely *his own* button-hook with the mother-of-pearl handle, I made a deliberate survey of the whole churchyard; and most of the names I had missed out of the signboards turned up for me once more on the tombstones. It was strange the feeling of almost glad recognition that came over me, in finding so many

familiar figures out of my childhood and youth all gathered
together in one place.

When the sexton came at eight to let me in, he found me ready
to be let out. 'How in the world had I got in!' 'Over the wall!'
'No! surely I couldn't mean that?' 'Why not?' 'Lords' sake, then,'
cried the man in real admiration, 'there is no end to you!' He
told me at parting, 'There is one man in this town, me'm, you
might like to see, James Robertson, your father's old servant.'
Our own old Jamie! he was waiter at 'The Star'—Good gracious!
—had returned to Haddington within the last year. 'Yes, indeed,'
I said, 'he must be sent to me at "The George" an hour hence,
and told only that a lady wanted him.'

It was still but eight o'clock, so I should have time to look at
Sunny Bank from the back gate, and streamed off in that direction. . . . Sunny Bank looked even lovelier 'in the light of a new
morning' than it had done in the evening dusk. A hedge of red
roses in full blow extended now from the house to the gate; and
I thought I might go in and gather one without evoking any—
beast. Once inside the gate, I passed easily to the idea of proceeding
as far as the back-door, just to ask the servant how they all were,
and leave compliments without naming myself; the servants
only would be astir so early. Well! when I had knocked at the
door with my finger, 'sharp but mannerly', it was opened by a
tidy maid-servant, exhibiting no more surprise than if I had been
the baker's boy! 'Are your ladies quite well?' I asked. 'Miss Jess
and Miss Catherine are quite well; Miss Donaldson rather com-
plaining. You are aware, me'm, that Mr Donaldson is dead.'
'Oh, dear, yes!' I said, thinking she meant Alexander. 'At what
hour do your ladies get up?' 'They are up, me'm, and done
breakfast. Will you walk round to the front door?' Goodness
gracious! should I 'walk round' or not? My own nerves had got
braced somewhat by the morning air; but *their* nerves!—how
would the sight of me thus 'promiscuously' operate on them?
'You had better go round and let me tell the ladies,' put in the
servant, as if in reply to my cogitations; 'what name shall I say?'
'None; I think perhaps my name would startle them more than
myself;—tell them someone they will be glad to see.' And so,
flinging the responsibility on Providence, I did 'go round', with
my heart thumping, 'like, like, like anything!' The maid-servant
met me at the front door, and conducted me to the drawing-
room; where was—nobody, but on a table lay a piece of black

bordered notepaper which explained to me that it was Mr Donaldson of London who was dead—the last brother—dead in these very days! I wished I had not come in, but it was out of time now. The door opened and showed me Miss Catherine changed into an old woman, and showed Miss Catherine me changed into one of—a certain age! She remained at the door, motionless, speechless, and I couldn't rise off my chair—at least I didn't; but when I saw her eyes, staring 'like watch faces', I said, 'Oh, Miss Catherine, don't be frightened at me!'—and then she quite shrieked 'Jeannie! Jeannie! Jeannie Welsh! my Jeannie! my Jeannie!' Oh, mercy! I shan't forget that scene in a hurry. I got her in my arms and kissed her into wits again; and then we both cried a little—naturally; both of us had enough since we last met to cry for. I explained to her 'how I was situated', as Mr C. would say, and that I was meaning to visit them after, like a Christian; and she found it all 'most wisely done, done like my own self'. Humph! poor Miss Catherine, it's little she knows of my own self, and perhaps the less the better! She told me about their brother's death, which had been sudden at the last. Supposing me still in London as usual, and that in London we hear of one another's deaths, they had been saying it was strange I did not write to them, and my godmother had remarked, 'It is not like her!' just while I was standing at their gate most likely, for it was 'the evening before, about dark', they had been speaking of me.

But again the door opened and showed Miss Jess. My godmother was keeping her bed 'with rheumatism' and grief. As I 'would really come back soon', it was settled to leave her quiet. They offered me breakfast, it was still on the table, but 'horrible was the thought' to me. It was all so solemn and doleful there that I should have heard every morsel going down my throat! Besides, I was engaged to breakfast with myself at the 'George'. So, with blessings for many days, I slipt away from them like a knotless thread.

My friend the cooper, espying me from his doorway on the road back, planted himself firmly in my path; 'if I would just compliment him with my name he would be *terribly* obliged; we had been uncommon comfortable together, and he must know what they called me!' I told him, and he neither died on the spot nor went mad; he looked pleased, and asked how many children I had had. 'None,' I told him. 'None?' in a tone of astonishment verging on horror. 'None at all? then what on earth had I been doing all this time?' 'Amusing myself,' I told him. He ran after me to beg I would give him a call on my return (I had spoken of returning) 'as he might be making something, belike, to send south with me, something small and of a fancy sort, liker myself than them I had bought.'

Breakfast stood ready for me at the inn, and was discussed in five minutes. Then I went to my bedroom to pack up. The chambermaid came to say a gentleman was asking for me. I flew down to my parlour and there was Jamie sure enough, Jamie to the life! and I threw my arms round his neck—that did I. He stood quite passive and quite pale, with great tears rolling down; it was minutes before he spoke, and then he said only, low under his breath, 'Mrs——Carlyle!' So nice he looked, and hardly a day older, and really as like 'a gentleman' as some lords; he had dressed himself in his Sunday clothes, for the occasion, and they were capital good ones. 'And you knew me, Jamie, at first sight?' I asked. 'Toot! we knew ye afore we seed ye.' 'Then you were told it was me?' 'No; they told us just we was to speak to a lady at the "George", and I knew it was Mrs Carlyle.' 'But how could you tell, dear Jamie?' 'Hoots! who else could it be?' Dear, funniest of created Jamies! He told me all sorts of particulars 'more profitable to the soul of man' than anything I should have got out of Mr Charteris in three years, never to say three weeks. But 'a waggon came in atween ten and eleven, and he must be stepping west. He was glad to have seen me looking so' (dropping his voice) 'stootish.'

And now there only remained to pay my bill and await the omnibus. I have that bill of 6s. 6d. in my writing-case, and shall keep it all my days. Another long look from the 'George Inn' window, and then into the shabby little omnibus again, where the faces of a lady next me and a gentleman opposite me tormented my memory without result.

In the railway carriage which I selected an old gentleman had taken his seat, and I recognized him at once as Mr Lea, the same who made the little obelisk which hangs in my bedroom at Chelsea. He was grown old like a golden pippin, merely 'crined', with the bloom upon him. I laid my hand on his arm, turning away my face, and said: 'Thank God here is one person I feel no difficulty about!' 'I don't know you,' he said, in his old blunt way; 'who are you?' 'Guess!' 'Was it you who got over the churchyard wall this morning? I saw a stranger lady climb the wall, and I said to myself, that's Jeannie Welsh! no other woman would climb the wall instead of going in at the gate. Are you Jeannie Welsh?' I owned the soft impeachment; then such shaking of hands, embracing even! But so soon as things had calmed down a little between us, Mr Lea laid his hand on my shoulder and said, as if pursuing knowledge under difficulties, 'Now tell me, my dear, why did you get over the wall instead of just asking for the key?'

And now . . . I was back into the present! and it is only in connection with the past that I can get up a sentiment for myself. The present Mrs Carlyle is—what shall I say?—detestable, upon my honour!

Rab And His Friends

DR JOHN BROWN

Four-and-thirty years ago, Bob Ainslie and I were coming up Infirmary Street from the High School, our heads together and our arms intertwisted, as only lovers and boys know how, or why.

When we got to the top of the street, and turned north, we espied a crowd at the Tron Church. 'A dog-fight!' shouted Bob, and was off; and so was I, both of us all but praying that it might not be over before we got up! And is not this boy-nature? and human nature too? and don't we all wish a house on fire not to be out before we see it? Dogs like fighting; old Isaac says they 'delight' in it, and for the best of all reasons; and boys are not cruel because they like to see the fight. They see three of the great cardinal virtues of dog or man—courage, endurance, and skill—in intense action. This is very different from a love of *making* dogs fight, and enjoying, and aggravating, and making gain by their pluck. A boy—be he ever so fond himself of fighting —if he be a good boy, hates and despises all this, but he would have run off with Bob and me fast enough: it is a natural, and a not wicked interest, that all boys and men have in witnessing intense energy in action.

Well, Bob and I are up, and find it is not over: a small thorough-bred white bull-terrier is busy throttling a large shepherd's dog, unaccustomed to war, but not to be trifled with. They are hard at it; the scientific little fellow doing his work in great style, his pastoral enemy fighting wildly, but with the sharpest of teeth and a great courage. Science and breeding, however, soon had their own; the Game Chicken, as the premature Bob called him, working his way up, took his final grip of poor Yarrow's throat —and he lay gasping and done for. Many were the means shouted out in mouthfuls, of the best possible ways of ending it. 'Water!' but there was none near, and many cried for it who might have got it from the well at Blackfriars Wynd. 'Bite the tail!' and a large, vague, benevolent, middle-aged man, more desirous than wise, with some struggle got the bushy end of *Yarrow's* tail into his ample mouth, and bit it with all his might. This was more than enough for the much-enduring, much-perspiring shepherd, who, with a gleam of joy over his broad visage, delivered a terrific facer upon our large, vague, benevolent, middle-aged friend—who went down like a shot.

Still the Chicken holds; death not far off. 'Snuff! a pinch of snuff!' observed a calm, highly-dressed young buck, with an eye-glass in his eye. 'Snuff, indeed!' growled the angry crowd, affronted and glaring. 'Snuff! a pinch of snuff!' again observes the buck, but with more urgency; whereupon were produced several open boxes, and from a mull which may have been at Culloden, he took a pinch, knelt down, and presented it to the nose of the Chicken. The laws of physiology and of snuff take their course; the Chicken sneezes, and Yarrow is free!

The young pastoral giant stalks off with Yarrow in his arms, —comforting him.

But the Bull-Terrier's blood is up, and his soul unsatisfied; he grips the first dog he meets, and discovering she is not a dog, in Homeric phrase, he makes a brief sort of *amende*, and is off. The boys, with Bob and me at their head, are after him: down Niddry Street he goes, bent on mischief; up the Cowgate like an arrow—Bob and I, and our small men, panting behind.

There, under the single arch of the South Bridge, is a huge mastiff, sauntering down the middle of the causeway, as if with his hands in his pockets: he is old, grey, brindled, as big as a little Highland bull, and has the Shakespearean dewlaps shaking as he goes.

The Chicken makes straight at him, and fastens on his throat. To our astonishment, the great creature does nothing but stand still, hold himself up, and roar—yes, roar; a long, serious, remonstrative roar. How is this? Bob and I are up to them. *He is muzzled!* The bailies had proclaimed a general muzzling, and his master, studying strength and economy mainly, had encompassed his huge jaws in a home-made apparatus, constructed out of the leather of some ancient breechin'. His mouth was open as far as it could; his lips curled up in rage—a sort of terrible grin; his teeth gleaming, ready, from out the darkness; the strap across his mouth tense as a bow-string; his whole frame stiff with indignation and surprise; his roar asking us all round, 'Did you ever see the like of this?' He looked a statue of anger and astonishment, done in Aberdeen granite.

We soon had a crowd: the Chicken held on. 'A knife!' cried Bob; and a cobbler gave him his knife: you know the kind of knife, worn away obliquely to a point, and always keen. I put its edge to the tense leather; it ran before it; and then!—one sudden jerk of that enormous head, a sort of dirty mist about his mouth, no noise—and the bright and fierce little fellow is dropped, limp, and dead. A solemn pause; this was more than any of us had bargained for. I turned the little fellow over, and saw he was quite dead: the mastiff had taken him by the small of the back like a rat, and broken it.

He looked down at his victim appeased, ashamed, and amazed; snuffed him all over, stared at him, and taking a sudden thought, turned round and trotted off. Bob took the dead dog up, and said, 'John, we'll bury him after tea.' 'Yes,' said I, and was off after the mastiff. He made up the Cowgate at a rapid swing; he had forgotten some engagement. He turned up the Candlemaker Row, and stopped at the Harrow Inn.

There was a carrier's cart ready to start, and a keen, thin, impatient, black-a-vised little man, his hand at his grey horse's head, looking about angrily for something. 'Rab, ye thief!' said he, aiming a kick at my great friend, who drew cringing up, and avoiding the heavy shoe with more agility than dignity, and watching his master's eye, slunk dismayed under the cart—his eyes down, and as much as he had of tail down too.

What a man this must be—thought I—to whom my tremendous hero turns tail! The carrier saw the muzzle hanging, cut and useless, from his neck, and I eagerly told him the story, which Bob and I always thought and still think, Homer or King David, or Sir Walter, alone were worthy to rehearse. The severe little man was mitigated, and condescended to say, 'Rab, ma man, puir Rabbie,'—whereupon the stump of a tail rose up, the ears were cocked, the eyes filled, and were comforted; the two friends were reconciled. 'Hupp!' and a stroke of the whip was given to Jess; and off went the three.

Bob and I buried the Game Chicken that night (we had not much of a tea) in the back-green of his house, in Melville Street, No. 17, with a considerable gravity and silence; and being at the time in the *Iliad*, and, like all boys, Trojans, we called him Hector of course.

Six years have passed—a long time, for a boy and a dog: Bob Ainslie is off to the wars; I am a medical student, and clerk at Minto House Hospital.

Rab I saw almost every week, on the Wednesday: and we had much pleasant intimacy. I found the way to his heart by frequent scratching of his huge head, and an occasional bone. When I did not notice him he would plant himself straight before me, and stand wagging that bud of a tail, and looking up with his head a little to the one side. His master I occasionally saw; he used to call me 'Maister John', but was laconic as any Spartan.

One fine October afternoon, I was leaving the hospital, when I saw the large gate open, and in walked Rab, with that great and easy saunter of his. He looked as if taking general possession of the place; like the Duke of Wellington entering a subdued city, satiated with victory and peace. After him came Jess, now white from age, with her cart; and in it a woman, carefully wrapped up—the carrier leading the horse anxiously, and looking back. When he saw me, James (for his name was James Noble) made a curt and grotesque 'boo', and said, 'Maister John, this is the mistress; she's got a trouble in her breest—some kind o' an income, we're thinking.'

By this time I saw the woman's face; she was sitting on a sack filled with straw, her husband's plaid round her, and his big coat, with its large white metal buttons, over her feet.

I never saw a more unforgettable face—pale, serious, *lonely*, delicate, sweet, without being at all what we call fine. She looked sixty, and had on a mutch, white as snow, with its black ribbon; her silvery, smooth hair setting off her dark grey eyes— eyes such as one sees only twice or thrice in a lifetime, full of suffering, full also of the overcoming of it: her eyebrows black and delicate, and her mouth firm, patient, and contented, which few mouths ever are.

As I have said, I never saw a more beautiful countenance, or one more subdued to settled quiet. 'Ailie,' said James, 'this is Maister John, the young doctor; Rab's freend, ye ken. We often speak aboot you, doctor.' She smiled, and made a movement, but said nothing; and prepared to come down, putting her plaid aside and rising. Had Solomon in all his glory been handing down the Queen of Sheba at his palace gate, he could not have done it more daintily, more tenderly, more like a gentleman, than did James the Howgate carrier, when he lifted down Ailie his wife. The contrast of his small, swarthy, weather-beaten, keen, worldly face to hers—pale, subdued, and beautiful—was something wonderful. Rab looked on, concerned and puzzled, but ready for anything that might turn up—were it to strangle the nurse, the porter, or even me. Ailie and he seemed great friends.

'As I was sayin', she's got a kind o' trouble in her breest, doctor; wull ye tak' a look at it?' We walked into the consulting-room, all four; Rab grim and comic, willing to be happy and confidential if cause could be shown, willing also to be the reverse, on the same terms. Ailie sat down, undid her open gown and her lawn handkerchief round her neck, and, without a word, showed me her right breast. I looked at and examined it carefully—she and James watching me, and Rab eyeing all three. What could I say? there it was, that had once been so soft, so shapely, so white, so gracious and bountiful, so 'full of all blessed conditions', hard as a stone, a centre of horrid pain, making that pale face, with its grey, lucid, reasonable eyes, and its sweet resolved mouth, express the full measures of suffering overcome. Why was that gentle, modest, sweet woman, clean and lovable, condemned by God to bear such a burden?

I got her away to bed. 'May Rab and me bide?' said James. '*You* may; and Rab, if he will behave himself.' 'I'se warrant he's do that, doctor'; and in slunk the faithful beast. I wish you could have seen him. There are no such dogs now. He belonged to a lost tribe. As I have said, he was brindled, and grey like Rubislaw granite; his hair short, hard, and close, like a lion's; his body thick-set, like a little bull—a sort of compressed Hercules of a dog. He must have been ninety pounds weight, at the least; he had a large blunt head; his muzzle black as night, his mouth blacker than any night, a tooth or two—being all he had—gleaming out of his jaws of darkness. His head was scarred with the records of old wounds, a sort of series of fields of battle all over it; one eye out, one ear cropped as close as was Archbishop

Leighton's father's; the remaining eye had the power of two; and above it, and in constant communication with it, was a tattered rag of an ear, which was for ever unfurling itself, like an old flag; and then that bud of a tail, about one inch long, if it could in any sense be said to be long, being as broad as long—the mobility, the instantaneousness of that bud were very funny and surprising, and its expressive twinklings and winkings, the inter-communications between the eye, the ear and it, were of the oddest and swiftest.

Rab had the dignity and simplicity of great size; and having fought his way all along the road to absolute supremacy, he was as mighty in his own line as Julius Caesar or the Duke of Wellington, and had the gravity of all great fighters.

You must have often observed the likeness of certain men to certain animals, and of certain dogs to men. Now I never looked at Rab without thinking of the great Baptist preacher, Andrew Fuller. The same large, heavy, menacing, combative, sombre, honest countenance, the same deep inevitable eye, the same look —as of thunder asleep but ready—neither a dog nor a man to be trifled with.

Next day, my master, the surgeon, examined Ailie. There was no doubt it must kill her, and soon. It could be removed—it might never return—it would give her speedy relief—she should have it done. She curtsied, looked at James, and said, 'When?' 'Tomorrow,' said the kind surgeon—a man of few words. She and James and Rab and I retired. I noticed that he and she spoke little, but seemed to anticipate everything in each other. The following day, at noon, the students came in, hurrying up the great stair, full of interest and talk. 'What's the case?' 'Which side is it?'

Don't think them heartless; they are neither better nor worse than you or I: they get over their professional horrors, and into their proper work; and in them pity—as an *emotion*, ending in itself or at best in tears and a long-drawn breath—lessens, while pity as a motive, is quickened and gains power and purpose. It is well for poor human nature that it is so.

The operating theatre is crowded; much talk and fun, and all the cordiality and stir of youth. The surgeon with his staff of assistants is there. In comes Ailie: one look at her quiets and abates the eager students. That beautiful old woman is too much for them; they sit down, and are dumb, and gaze at her. These rough boys feel the power of her presence. She walks in quickly, but without haste; dressed in her mutch, her neckerchief, her white dimity shortgown, her black bombazeen petticoat, showing her white worsted stockings and her carpet-shoes. Behind her was James with Rab. James sat down in the distance, and took that huge and noble head between his knees. Rab looked perplexed and dangerous; for ever cocking his ear and dropping it as fast.

Ailie stepped up on a seat, and laid herself on the table, as her friend the surgeon told her; arranged herself, gave a rapid look at James, shut her eyes, rested herself on me, and took my hand. The operation was at once begun; it was necessarily slow; and chloroform—one of God's best gifts to His suffering children —was then unknown. The surgeon did his work. The pale face showed its pain but was still and silent. Rab's soul was working within him; he saw that something strange was going on—blood flowing from his mistress, and she suffering; his ragged ear was up, and importunate; he growled and gave now and then a sharp impatient yelp; he would have liked to have done something to that man. But James had him firm, and gave him a *glower* from time to time; and an intimation of a possible kick;—all the better for James, it kept his eye and his mind off Ailie.

It is over: she is dressed, steps gently and decently down from the table, looks for James; then, turning to the surgeon and the students, she curtsies—and in a low, clear voice, begs their pardon if she has behaved ill. The students—all of us—wept like children; the surgeon happed her up carefully—and, resting on James and me, Ailie went to her room, Rab following. We put her to bed. James took off his heavy shoes, crammed with tackets, heel-capt, and toe-capt, and put them carefully under the table, saying, 'Maister John, I'm for nane o' yer strynge nurse bodies for Ailie. I'll be her nurse, and I'll gang aboot on my stock' soles as canny as pussy.' And so he did; and handy and clever, and swift and tender as any woman, was that horny-handed, snell, peremptory little man. Everything she got he gave her; he seldom slept, and often I saw his small shrewd eyes out of the darkness, fixed on her. As before, they spoke little.

Rab behaved well, never moving, showing us how meek and gentle he could be, and occasionally, in his sleep, letting us know that he was demolishing some adversary. He took a walk with me every day, generally to the Candlemaker Row; but he was sombre and mild; declined doing battle, though some fit cases offered, and indeed submitted to sundry indignities; and was always very ready to turn, and came faster back, and trotted up the stair with much lightness, and went straight to that door.

Jess, the mare, had been sent, with her weather-worn cart, to Howgate, and had doubtless her own dim and placid meditations and confusions on the absence of her master and Rab, and her unnatural freedom from the road and her cart.

For some days Ailie did well. The wound healed 'by the first intention'; for as James said, 'Oor Ailie's skin's ower clean to beil.' The students came in quiet and anxious, and surrounded her bed. She said she liked to see their young, honest faces. The surgeon dressed her, and spoke to her in his own short kind way, pitying her through his eyes, Rab and James outside the circle— Rab being now reconciled, and even cordial, and having made up his mind that as yet nobody required worrying, but, as you may suppose, *semper paratus*.

So far well: but, four days after the operation, my patient had a sudden and long shivering, a 'groosin' ', as she called it. I saw her soon after; her eyes were too bright, her cheek coloured: she was restless, and ashamed of being so; the balance was lost; mischief had begun. On looking at the wound, a blush of red told the secret: her pulse was rapid, her breathing anxious and quick, she wasn't herself, as she said, and was vexed at her restlessness. We tried what we could. James did everything, was everything; never in the way, never out of it; Rab subsided under the table into a dark place, and was motionless, all but his eye, which followed everyone. Ailie got worse; began to wander in her mind, gently; was more demonstrative in her ways to James, rapid in her questions, and sharp at times. He was vexed, and said, 'She was never that way afore; no, never.' For a time she knew her head was wrong, and was always asking our pardon —the dear, gentle old woman; then delirium set in strong, without pause. She sang bits of old songs and Psalms, stopping suddenly, mingling the Psalms of David, and the diviner words of his Son and Lord, with homely odds and ends and scraps of ballads.

Nothing more touching, or in a sense more strangely beautiful, did I ever witness. Her tremulous, rapid, affectionate, eager Scotch voice—the swift, aimless, bewildered mind, the baffled utterance, the bright and perilous eye; some wild words, some household cares, something for James, the names of the dead, Rab called rapidly and in a 'fremyt' voice, and he starting up, surprised, and slinking off as if he were to blame somehow, or had been dreaming he heard. Many eager questions and beseechings which James and I could make nothing of, and on which she seemed to set her all, and then sink back ununderstood. It was very sad, but better than many things that are not called sad. James hovered about, put out and miserable, but active and exact as ever; read to her, when there was a lull, short bits from the Psalms, prose and metre, chanting the latter in his own rude and serious way, showing great knowledge of the fit words, bearing up like a man, and doating over her as his 'ain Ailie'. 'Ailie, ma woman!' 'Ma ain bonnie wee dawtie!'

The end was drawing on: the golden bowl was breaking; the silver cord was fast being loosed—that *animula blandula*, *vagula*, *hospes*, *comesque*, was about to flee. The body and soul—companions for sixty years—were being sundered, and taking leave. She was walking alone, through the valley of that shadow, into which one day we must all enter—and yet she was not alone, for we know whose rod and staff were comforting her.

One night she had fallen quiet, and as we hoped, asleep; her eyes were shut. We put down the gas, and sat watching her. Suddenly she sat up in bed, and taking a bed-gown which was lying on it, rolled up, she held it eagerly to her breast—to the right side. We could see her eyes bright with a surprising tenderness and joy, bending over this bundle of clothes. She held it as a woman holds her sucking child; opening out her nightgown impatiently, and holding it close, and brooding over it, and murmuring foolish little words, as over one whom his mother comforteth, and who sucks and is satisfied. It was pitiful and strange to see her wasted dying look, keen and yet vague—her immense love.

'Preserve me!' groaned James, giving way. And then she rocked back and forward, as if to make it sleep, hushing it, and wasting on it her infinite fondness. 'Wae's me, doctor; I declare she's thinkin' it's that bairn.' 'What bairn?' 'The only bairn we ever had; our wee Mysie, and she's in the Kingdom, forty years and mair.' It was plainly true: the pain in the breast, telling its urgent story to a bewildered, ruined brain, was misread and mistaken; it suggested to her the uneasiness of a breast full of milk,

6

and then the child; and so again once more they were together, and she had her ain wee Mysie in her bosom.

This was the close. She sank rapidly: the delirium left her; but, as she whispered, she was 'clean silly'; it was the lightening before the final darkness. After having for sometime lain still—her eyes shut, she said 'James!' He came close to her, and lifting up her calm, clear, beautiful eyes, she gave him a long look, turned to me kindly but shortly, looked for Rab but could not see him, then turned to her husband again, as if she would never leave off looking, shut her eyes, and composed herself. She lay for some time breathing quick, and passed away so gently, that when we thought she was gone, James, in his old-fashioned way, held the mirror to her face. After a long pause, one small spot of dimness was breathed out; it vanished away, and never returned, leaving the blank clear darkness of the mirror without a stain. 'What is our life? it is even a vapour, which appeareth for a little time, and then vanisheth away.'

Rab all this time had been full awake and motionless: he came forward beside us; Ailie's hand, which James had held, was hanging down; it was soaked with his tears; Rab licked it all over carefully, looked at her, and returned to his place under the table.

James and I sat, I don't know how long, but for some time—saying nothing: he started up abruptly, and with some noise went to the table, and putting his right fore and middle finger each into a shoe, pulled them out, and put them on, breaking one of the leather latchets, and muttering in anger, 'I never did the like o' that afore!'

I believe he never did; nor after either. 'Rab!' he said roughly, and pointing with his thumb to the bottom of the bed. Rab leapt up, and settled himself; his head and eye to the dead face. 'Maister John, ye'll wait for me,' said the carrier; and disappeared in the darkness, thundering downstairs in his heavy shoes. I ran to a front window: there he was, already round the house, and out at the gate, fleeing like a shadow.

I was afraid about him, and yet not afraid; so I sat down beside Rab, and being wearied, fell asleep. I awoke from a sudden noise outside. It was November, and there had been a heavy fall of snow. Rab was *in statu quo*; he heard the noise too, and plainly knew it, but never moved. I looked out; and there, at the gate, in the dim morning—for the sun was not up, was Jess and the cart—a cloud of steam rising from the old mare. I did not see

James; he was already at the door, and came up the stairs, and met me. It was less than three hours since he left, and he must have posted out—who knows how?—to Howgate, full nine miles off; yoked Jess, and driven her astonished into town. He had an armful of blankets, and was streaming with perspiration. He nodded to me, spread out on the floor two pair of clean old blankets having at their corners '*A. G. 1796*' in large letters in red worsted. These were the initials of Alison Graeme, and James may have looked in at her from without—himself unseen but not unthought of—when he was 'wat, wat, and weary', and after having walked many a mile over the hills, may have seen her sitting, while 'a' the lave were sleeping' and by the firelight working her name on the blankets, for her ain James's bed.

He motioned Rab down, and taking his wife in his arms, laid her in the blankets, and happed her carefully and firmly up, leaving the face uncovered; and then lifting her, he nodded again sharply to me, and with a resolved but utterly miserable face, strode along the passage, and downstairs, followed by Rab. I followed with a light; but he didn't need it. I went out, holding stupidly the candle in my hand in the calm frosty air; we were soon at the gate. I could have helped him, but I saw he was not to be meddled with, and he was strong, and did not need it. He laid her down as tenderly, as safely, as he had lifted her out ten days before—as tenderly as when he had her first in his arms when she was only 'A. G.'—sorted her, leaving that beautiful sealed face open to the heavens; and then taking Jess by the head, he moved away. He did not notice me, neither did Rab, who presided behind the cart.

I stood till they passed through the long shadow of the College, and turned up Nicolson Street. I heard the solitary cart sound through the streets and die away and come again; and I returned, thinking of that company going up Liberton Brae, then along Roslin Muir, the morning light touching the Pentlands and making them like on-looking ghosts; then down the hill through Auchindinny woods, past 'haunted Woodhouselee'; and as daybreak came sweeping up the bleak Lammermuirs, and fell on his own door, the company would stop, and James would take the key and lift Ailie up again, laying her on her own bed, and, having put Jess up, would return with Rab and shut the door.

James buried his wife, with his neighbours mourning, Rab inspecting the solemnity from a distance. It was snow, and that black ragged hole would look strange in the midst of the swelling spotless cushion of white. James looked after everything; then rather suddenly fell ill and took to bed; was insensible when the doctor came, and soon died. A sort of low fever was prevailing in the village, and his want of sleep, his exhaustion, and his misery, made him apt to take it. The grave was not difficult to reopen. A fresh fall of snow had again made all things white and smooth; Rab once more looked on, and slunk home to the stable.

And what of Rab? I asked for him next week at the new carrier who got the goodwill of James's business, and was now master of Jess and her cart. 'How's Rab?' He put me off, and said rather rudely, 'What's *your* business wi' the dowg?' I was not to be so put off. 'Where's Rab?' He, getting confused and red, and inter-meddling with his hair, said, ' 'Deed, sir, Rab's deid.' 'Dead! what did he die of?' 'Weel, sir,' said he, getting redder, 'he didna exactly dee; he was killed. I had to brain him wi' a rack-pin; there was nae doin' wi' him. He lay in the treviss wi' the mear, and wadna come oot. I tempit him wi' kail and meat, but he wad tak naething, and keepit me frae feedin' the beast, and he was aye gur gurrin', and grup gruppin' me by the legs. I was laith to make awa wi' the auld dowg, his like wasna atween this and Thornhill—but 'deed, sir, I could dae naething else.' I believed him. Fit end for Rab, quick and complete. His teeth and his friends gone, why should he keep the peace and be civil?

He was buried in the braeface, near the burn, the children of the village, his companions, who used to make very free with him and sit on his ample stomach, as he lay half-asleep at the door in the sun—watching the solemnity.

6

The Bodies

GEORGE DOUGLAS
BROWN

In every little Scotch community there is a distinct type known as the 'bodie'. 'What does he do, that man?' you may ask, and the answer will be, 'Really, I could hardly tell ye what he does—he's just a bodie!' The 'bodie' may be a gentleman of independent means (a hundred a year from the Funds) fussing about in spats and light check breeches; or he may be a jobbing gardener; but he is equally a 'bodie'. The chief occupation of his idle hours (and his hours are chiefly idle) is the discussion of his neighbour's affairs. He is generally an 'auld residenter', great, therefore, at the redding up of pedigrees. He can tell you exactly, for instance, how it is that young Pin-oe's taking geyly to the dram; for his grandfather, it seems, was a terrible man for the drink—ou, just terrible. Why, he went to bed with a full jar of whisky once, and when he left it he was dead, and it was empty. So, ye see, that's the reason on't.

The genus 'bodie' is divided into two species—the 'harmless bodies' and the 'nesty bodies'. The bodies of Barbie mostly belonged to the second variety. Johnny Coe and Tam Wylie and the baker were decent enough fellows in their way, but the others were the sons of scandal. Gourlay spoke of them as a 'wheen damned auld wives'. But Gourlay, to be sure, was not an impartial witness.

The Bend o' the Brae was the favourite stance of the bodies: here they forgathered every day to pass judgment on the town's affairs. And, indeed, the place had many things to recommend it. Among the chief it was within an easy distance of the Red Lion, farther up the street, to which it was really very convenient to adjourn nows and nans. Standing at the Bend o' the Brae, too, you could look along two roads to the left and right, or down upon the Cross beneath, and the three low streets that guttered away from it. Or you might turn and look up Main Street, and past the side of the Square, to the House with the Green Shutters, the highest in the town. The Bend o' the Brae, you will gather, was a fine post for observation. It had one drawback, true: if Gourlay turned to the right in his gig he disappeared in a moment, and you could never be sure where he was off to. But even that afforded matter for pleasing speculation which often lasted half an hour.

It was about nine o'clock when Gourlay and Gilmour quarrelled in the yard, and that was the hour when the bodies forgathered for their morning dram.

'Good moarning, Mr Wylie!' said the Provost.

When the Provost wished you good morning, with a heavy civic eye, you felt sure it was going to be good.

'Mornin', Provost, mornin'! Fine weather for the fields,' said Tam, casting a critical glance at the blue dome in which a soft, white-bosomed cloud floated high above the town. 'If this weather hauds, it'll be a blessing for us poor farming bodies.'

Tam was a wealthy old hunks, but it suited his humour to refer to himself constantly as a 'poor farming bodie'. And he dressed in accordance with his humour. His clean old crab-apple face was always grinning at you from over a white-sleeved moleskin waistcoat, as if he had been no better than a breaker of road-metal.

'Faith ay!' said the Provost, cunning and quick; 'fodder should be cheap'—and he shot the covetous glimmer of a bargain-making eye at Mr Wylie.

Tam drew himself up. He saw what was coming.

'We're needing some hay for the burgh horse,' said the Provost. 'Ye'll be willing to sell at fifty shillings the ton, since it's like to be so plentiful.'

'Oh,' said Tam solemnly, 'that's on-possible! Gourlay's seeking the three pound! and where he leads we maun a' gang. Gourlay sets the tune, and Barbie dances till't.'

That was quite untrue so far as the speaker was concerned. It took a clever man to make Tam Wylie dance to his piping. But

Thomas, the knave, knew that he could always take a rise out of
the Provost by cracking up the Gourlays, and that to do it now
was the best way of fobbing him off about the hay.

'Gourlay!' muttered the Provost, in disgust. And Tam winked
at the baker.

'Losh,' said Sandy Toddle, 'yonder's the Free Kirk minister
going past the Cross! Where'll *he* be off till at this hour of the
day? He's not often up so soon.'

'They say he sits late studying,' said Johnny Coe.

'H'mph, studying!' grunted Tam Brodie, a big, heavy, wall-
cheeked man, whose little, side-glancing eyes seemed always
alert for scandal amid the massive insolence of his smooth face.
'I see few signs of studying in *him*. He's noathing but a stink wi'
a skin on't.'

T. Brodie was a very important man, look you, and wrote
'Leather Mercht.' above his door, though he cobbled with his
own hands. He was a staunch Conservative, and down on the
Dissenters.

'What road'th he taking?' lisped Deacon Allardyce, craning
past Brodie's big shoulder to get a look.

'He's stoppit to speak to Widow Wallace. What will he be
saying to *her*?'

'She's a greedy bodie that Mrs Wallace; I wouldna wonder
but she's speiring him for bawbees.'

'Will he take the Skeighan Road, I wonder?'

'Or the Fechars?'

'He's a great man for gathering gowans and other sic trash.
He's maybe for a dander up the burn juist. They say he's a great
botanical man.'

'Ay,' said Brodie, 'paidling in a burn's the ploy for him. He's
a weanly gowk.'

'A-a-ah!' protested the baker, who was a Burnsomaniac,
'there's waur than a walk by the bank o' a bonny burn. Ye ken
what Mossgiel said:

> "*The Muse nae poet ever fand her,*
> *Till by himsel' he learned to wander,*
> *Adown some trottin' burn's meander,*
> *And no thick lang;*
> *Oh sweet to muse and pensive ponder*
> *A heartfelt sang.*" '

Poetical quotations, however, made the Provost uncomfortable. 'Ay,' he said dryly in his throat; 'verra good, baker, verra good! —Who's yellow doag's that? I never saw the beast about the town before!'

'Nor me either. It's a perfect stranger!'

'It's like a herd's doag!'

'Man, you're right! That's just what it will be. The morn's Fleckie lamb fair, and some herd or other'll be in about the town.'

'He'll be drinking in some public-house, I'se warrant, and the doag will have lost him.'

'Imph, that'll be the way o't.'

'I'm demned if he hasn't taken the Skeighan Road!' said Sandy Toddle, who had kept his eye on the minister. Toddle's accent was a varying quality. When he remembered he had been a packman in England, it was exceedingly fine. But he often forgot.

'The Skeighan Road! the Skeighan Road! Who'll he be going to see in that airt? Will it be Templandmuir?'

'Gosh, it canna be Templandmuir; he was there no later than yestreen!'

'Here's a man coming down the brae!' announced Johnny Coe, in a solemn voice, as if a man 'coming down the brae' was something unusual. In a moment every head was turned to the hill.

'What's yon he's carrying on his shoulder?' pondered Brodie.

'It looks like a boax,' said the Provost slowly, bending every effort of eye and mind to discover what it really was. He was giving his profoundest cogitations to the 'boax'.

'It *is* a boax! But who is it, though? I canna make him out.'

'Dod, I canna tell either; his head's so bent with his burden!'

At last the man, laying his 'boax' on the ground, stood up to ease his spine, so that his face was visible.

'Losh, it's Jock Gilmour, the orra man at Gourlay's! What'll *he* be doing out on the street at this hour of the day? I thocht he was always busy on the premises! Will Gourlay be sending him off with something to somebody? But no; that canna be. He would have sent it with the carts.'

'I'll wager ye,' cried Johnny Coe quickly, speaking more loudly than usual in the animation of discovery—'I'll wager ye Gourlay has quarrelled him and put him to the door!'

'Man, you're right! That'll just be it, that'll just be it! Ay, ay—faith ay—and yon'll be his kist he's carrying! Man, you're right, Mr Coe; you have just put your finger on't. We'll hear news *this* morning.'

They edged forward to the middle of the road, the Provost in front, to meet Gilmour coming down.

'Ye've a heavy burden this morning, John,' said the Provost graciously.

'No wonder, sir,' said Gilmour, with big-eyed solemnity, and set down the chest; 'it's no wonder, seeing that I'm carrying my a-all.'

'Ay, man, John. How's that na?'

To be the centre of interest and the object of gracious condescension was balm to the wounded feelings of Gilmour. Gourlay had lowered him, but his reception restored him to his own good opinion. He was usually called 'Jock' (except by his mother, to whom, of course, he was 'oor Johnny'), but the best merchants in the town were addressing him as 'John'. It was a great occasion. Gilmour expanded in gossip beneath its influence benign.

He welcomed, too, this first and fine opportunity of venting his wrath on the Gourlays.

'Oh, I just telled Gourlay what I thocht of him, and took the door ahint me. I let him have it hot and hardy, I can tell ye. He'll no forget *me* in a hurry,'—Gilmour bawled angrily, and nodded his head significantly, and glared fiercely, to show what good cause he had given Gourlay to remember him—'he'll no forget *me* for a month of Sundays.'

'Ay, man, John, what did ye say till him?'

'Na, man, what did he say to you?'

'Wath he angry, Dyohn?'

'How did the thing begin?'

'Tell us, man, John.'

'What was it all about, John?'

'Was Mrs Gourlay there?'

Bewildered by this pelt of questions, Gilmour answered the last that hit his ear. 'There, ay; faith, she was there. It was her was the cause o't.'

'D'ye tell me that, John? Man, you surprise me. I would have thocht the thowless trauchle hadna the smeddum left to interfere.'

'Oh, it was yon boy of hers. He's aye swaggerin' aboot, interferin' wi' folk at their wark—he follows his faither's example in that, for as the auld cock craws the young ane learns—and his mither's that daft aboot him that ye daurna give a look! He came in my road when I was sweeping out the close, and some o' the dirty jaups splashed about his shins. But was I to blame for that? —ye maun walk wide o' a whalebone besom if ye dinna want to be splashed. Afore I kenned where I was, he up wi' a dirty washing-clout and slashed me in the face wi't! I hit him a thud in the ear—as wha wadna? Out come his mither like a fury, skirling about *her* hoose, and *her* servants, and *her* weans. "Your servant!" says I—"your servant! You're a nice-looking trollop to talk aboot servants," says I.'

'Did ye really, John?'

'Man, that wath bauld o' ye.'

'And what did *she* say?'

'Oh, she just kept skirling! And then, to be sure, Gourlay must come out and interfere! But I telled him to his face what I thocht of *him*! "The best Gourlay that ever dirtied leather," says I, " 's no gaun to make dirt of me," says I.'

'Ay, man, Dyohn!' lisped Deacon Allardyce, with bright and eagerly inquiring eyes. 'And what did he thay to that na? *That* wath a dig for him! I'the warrant he wath angry.'

'Angry? He foamed at the mouth! But I up and says to him, "I have had enough o' you," says I, "you and your Hoose wi' the Green Shutters," says I. "You're no' fit to have a decent servant," says I. "Pay *me my* wages, and I'll be redd o' ye," says I. And wi' that I flang my kist on my shoulder and slapped the gate ahint me.'

'And *did* he pay ye your wages?' Tam Wylie probed him slyly, with a sideward glimmer in his eye.

'Ah, well, no—not exactly,' said Gilmour, drawing in. 'But I'll get them right enough for a' that. He'll no get the better o' *me.*' Having grounded unpleasantly on the question of the wages, he thought it best to be off ere the bloom was dashed from his importance, so he shouldered his chest and went. The bodies watched him down the street.

'He's a lying brose, that,' said the baker. 'We a' ken what Gourlay is. He would have flung Gilmour out by the scruff o' the neck if he had daured to set his tongue against him!'

'Faith, that's so,' said Tam Wylie and Johnny Coe together.

But the others were divided between their perception of the fact and their wish to believe that Gourlay had received a thrust or two. At other times they would have been the first to scoff at

Gilmour's swagger. Now their animus against Gourlay prompted them to back it up.

'Oh, I'm not so sure of tha-at, baker,' cried the Provost, in the false, loud voice of a man defending a position which he knows to be unsound. 'I'm no' so sure of that at a-all. A-a-h, mind ye,' he drawled persuasively, 'he's a hardy fallow, that Gilmour. I've no doubt he gied Gourlay a good dig or two. Let us howp they will do him good.'

'Shall we adjourn?' said Brodie, when they had watched Jock Gilmour out of sight. He pointed across his shoulder to the Red Lion.

'Better noat just now,' said the Provost, nodding in slow authority—'better noat just now! I'm very anxious to see Gourlay about yon matter we were speaking of, doan't ye understa-and? But I'm determined not to go to his house! On the other hand, if we go into the Red Lion the now, we may miss him on the street. We'll noat have loang to wait, though; he'll be down the town directly, to look at the horses he has at the gerse out the Fechars Road. But *I'm* talling ye, I simply will noat go to his house—to put up with a wheen damned insults!' he puffed in angry recollection.

'To tell the truth,' said Wylie, 'I don't like to call upon Gourlay either. I'm aware of his eyes on my back when I slink beaten through his gate, and I feel that my hurdies are wanting in dignity!'

'Huh!' spluttered Brodie, 'that never affects me. I come stunting out in a bleeze of wrath and slam the yett ahint me!'

'Oh, well,' said the Deacon, 'that'th one way of being dignified.'

'I'm afraid,' said Sandy Toddle, 'that he won't be in a very good key to consider our request this morning, after his quarrel with Gilmour.'

'No,' said the Provost; 'he'll be blazing angry—It's most unfortunate. But we maun try to get his consent, be his temper what it will. It's a matter of importance to the town, doan't ye see, and if he refuses we simply can-noat proceed wi' the improvement.'

'It was Gilmour's jibe at the House wi' the Green Shutters that would anger him the most, for it's the perfect god of his idolatry. Eh, sirs, he has wasted an awful money upon yon house!'

'Wasted's the word!' said Brodie, with a blatant laugh.
'Wasted's the word! They say he has verra little lying cash! And
I shouldna be surprised at all. For, ye see, Gibson the builder
diddled him owre the building o't.'

'Oh, I'se warrant Cunning Johnny would get the better of an
ass like Gourlay. But how in particular, Mr Brodie? Have ye
heard ainy details?'

'I've been on the track o' the thing for a while back, but it
was only yestreen I had the proofs o't. It was Robin Wabster
that telled me. He's a jouking bodie, Robin, and he was ahint a
dike up Skeighan Road when Gibson and Gourlay forgathered
—they stoppit just forenenst him! Gourlay began to curse at
the size of Gibson's bill, but Cunning Johnny kenned the way
to get round him brawly. "Mr Gourlay," says he, "there's not a
thing in your house that a man in your poseetion can afford to
be without, and ye needn't expect the best house in Barbie for
an auld song!" And Gourlay was pacified at once! It appeared
frae their crack, however, that Gibson has diddled him tremendous. "Verra well then," Robin heard Gourlay cry, "you must
allow me a while ere I pay that!" I wager, for a' sae muckle as
he's made of late, that his balance at the bank's a sma' yin.'

'More thyow than thusbstanth,' said the Deacon.

'Well, I'm sure!' said the Provost, 'he needn't have built such
a gra-and house to put a slut of a wife like yon in!'

'I was surprised,' said Sandy Toddle, 'to hear her firing up.
I wouldn't have thought she had the spirit, or that Gourlay
would have come to her support!'

'Oh,' said the Provost, 'it wasn't her he was thinking of! It
was his own pride, the brute. He leads the woman the life of a
doag. I'm surprised that he ever married her!'

'I ken fine how he married her,' said Johnny Coe. 'I was
acquainted wi' her faither, auld Tenshillingland, owre at Fechars
—a grand farmer he was, wi' land o' his nain, and a gey pickle
bawbees. It was the bawbees, and not the woman, that Gourlay
went after! It was *her* money, as ye ken, that set him on his feet,
and made him such a big man. He never cared a preen for *her*,
and then when she proved a dirty trollop, he couldna endure
her look! That's what makes him so sore upon her now. And
yet I mind her a braw lass, too,' said Johnny the sentimentalist,
'a braw lass she was,' he mused, 'wi' fine, brown glossy hair, I
mind, and—ochonee! ochonee!—as daft as a yett in a windy day.

She had a cousin, Jenny Wabster, that dwelt in Tenshillingland than, and mony a summer nicht up the Fechars Road, when ye smelled the honeysuckle in the gloaming, I have heard the two o' them tee-heeing owre the lads thegither, skirling in the dark and lauching to themselves. They were of the glaiket kind ye can always hear loang before ye see. Jock Allan (that has done so well in Embro) was a herd at Tenshillingland than, and he likit her, and I think she likit him; but Gourlay came wi' his gig and whisked her away. She doesna lauch sae muckle now, puir bodie! But a braw lass she—'

'It's you maun speak to Gourlay, Deacon,' said the Provost, brushing aside the reminiscent Coe.

'How can it be that, Provost? It'th *your* place, surely. You're the head of the town!'

When Gourlay was to be approached there was always a competition for who should be hindmost.

'Yass, but you know perfectly well, Deacon, that I cannot thole the look of him. I simply cannot thole the look. And he knows it too. The thing'll gang smash at the outset—*I'm* talling ye, now—it'll go smash at the outset if it's left to me. And than, ye see, you have a better way of approaching folk!'

'Ith that tho?' said the Deacon dryly. He shot a suspicious glance to see if the Provost was guying him.

'Oh, it must be left to you, Deacon,' said the baker and Tam Wylie in a breath.

'Certainly, it maun be left to the Deacon,' assented Johnny Coe, when he saw how the others were giving their opinion.

'Tho be it, then,' snapped the Deacon.

'Here he comes,' said Sandy Toddle.

Gourlay came down the street towards them, his chest big, his thumbs in the armholes of his waistcoat. He had the power of staring steadily at those whom he approached without the slightest sign of recognition or intelligence appearing in his eyes. As he marched down upon the bodies he fixed them with a wide-open glower that was devoid of every expression but courageous steadiness. It gave a kind of fierce vacancy to his look.

The Deacon limped forward on his thin shanks to the middle of the road.

'It'th a fine morning, Mr Gourlay,' he simpered.

'There's noathing wrong with the morning,' grunted Gourlay, as if there was something wrong with the Deacon.

'We wath wanting to thee ye on a very important matter, Mithter Gourlay,' lisped the Deacon, smiling up at the big man's face, with his head on one side, and rubbing his fingers in front of him. 'It'th a matter of the common good, you thee; and we all agreed that we should speak to *you*, ath the foremost merchant of the town!'

Allardyce meant his compliment to fetch Gourlay. But Gourlay knew his Allardyce, and was cautious. It was well to be on your guard when the Deacon was complimentary. When his language was most flowery there was sure to be a serpent hidden in it somewhere. He would lisp out an innocent remark and toddle away, and Gourlay would think nothing of the matter till a week afterwards, perhaps, when something would flash a light; then 'Damn him, did he mean "*that*"?' he would seethe, starting back and staring at the '*that*' while his fingers strangled the air in place of the Deacon.

He glowered at the Deacon now till the Deacon blinked.

'You thee, Mr Gourlay,' Allardyce shuffled uneasily, 'it'th for your own benefit just ath much ath ourth. We were thinking of you ath well ath ourthelves! Oh yeth, oh yeth!'

'Ay, man!' said Gourlay, 'that was kind of ye! I'll be the first man in Barbie to get ainy benefit from the fools that mismanage our affairs.'

The gravel grated beneath the Provost's foot. The atmosphere was becoming electric, and the Deacon hastened to the point.

'You thee, there'th a fine natural supply of water—a perfect reservore the Provost sayth—on the braeface just above *your* garden, Mr Gourlay. Now, it would be easy to lead that water down and alang through all the gardenth on the high side of Main Street—and, 'deed, it might feed a pump at the Cross, too, to supply the lower portionth o' the town. It would really be a grai-ait convenience. Every man on the high side o' Main Street would have a running spout at his own back door! If your garden didna run tho far back, Mr Gourlay, and ye hadna the muckle land about your place'—*that* should fetch him, thought the Deacon—'if it werena for that, Mr Gourlay, we could easily lead the water round to the other gardenth without interfering with your property. But, ath it ith, we simply cannoat move without ye. The water must come through your garden, if it comes at a-all.'

'The most o' you important men live on the high side o' Main

Street,' birred Gourlay. 'Is it the poor folk at the Cross, or your ain bits o' back doors that you're thinking o'?'

'Oh—oh, Mr Gourlay!' protested Allardyce, head flung back, and palms in air, to keep the thought of self-interest away, 'oh—oh, Mr Gourlay! We're thinking of noathing but the common good, I do assure ye!'

'Ay, man! You're dis-in-ter-ested!' said Gourlay, but he stumbled on the big word and spoiled the sneer. That angered him, and, 'It's likely,' he rapped out, 'that I'll allow the land round *my* house to be howked and trenched and made a mudhole of to oblige a wheen things like you!'

'Oh—oh, but think of the convenience to uth—eh—eh—I mean to the common good,' said Allardyce.

'I howked wells for myself,' snapped Gourlay. 'Let others do the like.'

'Oh, but we haven't all the enterprithe of you, Mr Gourlay. You'll surely accommodate the town.'

'I'll see the town damned first,' said Gourlay, and passed on his steady way.

The bodies watched Gourlay in silence until he was out of earshot. Then, 'It's monstrous!' the Provost broke out in solemn anger; 'I declare it's perfectly monstrous! But I believe we could get Pow-ers to compel him. Yass; I believe we could get Pow-ers. I do believe we could get Pow-ers.'

The Provost was fond of talking about 'Pow-ers', because it implied that he was intimate with the great authorities who might delegate such 'Pow-ers' to him. To talk of 'Pow-ers', mysteriously, was a tribute to his own importance. He rolled the word on his tongue as if he enjoyed the sound of it.

On the Deacon's cheek-bones two red spots flamed, round and big as a Scotch penny. His was the hurt silence of the baffled diplomatist, to whom a defeat means reflections on his own ability.

'Demn him!' he skirled, following the solid march of his enemy with fiery eyes.

Never before had his deaconship been heard to swear. Tam Wylie laughed at the shrill oath till his eyes were buried in his merry wrinkles, a suppressed snirt, a continuous gurgle in the throat and nose, in beaming survey the while of the withered old creature dancing in his rage. (It was all a good joke to Tam, because, living on the outskirts of the town, he had no spigot of his own to feed.) The Deacon turned the eyes of hate on him. Demn Wylie too—what was he laughing at!

'Oh, I dare say you could have got round him!' he snapped.

'In my opinion, Allardyce,' said the baker, 'you mismanaged the whole affair. Yon wasna the way to approach him!'

'It'th a pity you didna try your hand, then, I'm sure! No doubt a clever man like *you* would have worked wonderth!'

So the bodies wrangled among themselves. Somehow or other Gourlay had the knack of setting them by the ears. It was not till they hit on a common topic of their spite in railing at him that they became a band of brothers and a happy few.

'Whisht!' said Sandy Toddle suddenly: 'here's his boy!'

John was coming towards them on his way to school. The bodies watched him as he passed, with the fixed look men turn on a boy of whose kinsmen they were talking even now. They affect a stony and deliberate regard, partly to include the newcomer in their critical survey of his family, and partly to banish from their own eyes any sign that they have just been running down his people. John, as quick as his mother to feel, knew in a moment they were watching *him*. He hung his head sheepishly and blushed, and the moment he was past he broke into a nervous trot, the bag of books bumping on his back as he ran.

'He's getting a big boy, that son of Gourlay's,' said the Provost, 'how oald will he be?'

'He's approaching twelve,' said Johnny Coe, who made a point of being able to supply such news because it gained him consideration where he was otherwise unheeded. 'He was born the day the brig on the Fleckie Road gaed down, in the year o' the great flood; and since the great flood it's twelve year come Lammas. Rab Tosh o' Fleckie's wife was heavy-footed at the time, and Doctor Munn had been a' nicht wi' her, and when he cam to Barbie Water in the morning it was roaring wide frae bank to brae; where the brig should have been there was naething but the swashing of the yellow waves. Munn had to drive a' the way round to the Fechars brig, and in parts o' the road the water was so deep that it lapped his horse's belly-band. A' this time Mrs Gourlay was skirling in her pains and praying to God she micht dee. Gourlay had been a great crony o' Munn's, but he quarrelled him for being late; he had trysted him, ye see, for the occasion, and he had been twenty times at the yett to look for him. Ye ken how little he would stomach that; he was ready to burst wi' anger. Munn, mad for the want of sleep and wat to the bane, swure back at him; and than Gourlay wadna let him near his wife! Ye mind what an awful day it was; the thunder roared as if the heavens were tumbling on the world, and the lichtnin' sent the trees daudin' on the roads, and folk hid below their beds and prayed—they thocht it was the Judgment! But Gourlay rammed his black stepper in the shafts and drave like the devil o' hell to Skeighan Drone, where there was a young doctor. The lad was feared to come, but Gourlay swore by God that he should, and he garred him. In a' the countryside driving like his that day was never kenned or heard tell o'; they were back within the hour! I saw them gallop up Main Street; lichtnin' struck the ground before them; the young doctor covered his face wi' his hands, and the horse nichered wi' fear and tried to wheel, but Gourlay stood up in the gig and lashed him on through the fire. It was thocht for lang that Mrs Gourlay would die; and she was never the same woman after. Atweel, ay, sire, Gourlay has that morning's work to blame for the poor wife he had now. Him and Munn never spoke to each other again, and Munn died within the twelvemonth—he got his death that morning on the Fleckie Road. But, for a' so pack's they had been, Gourlay never looked near him.'

Coe had told his story with enjoying gusto, and had told it well —for Johnny, though constantly snubbed by his fellows, was in many ways the ablest of them all. His voice and manner drove it home. They knew, besides, he was telling what himself had seen. For they knew he was lying prostrate with fear in the open smiddy-shed from the time Gourlay went to Skeighan Drone to the time that he came back, and that he had seen him both come and go. They were silent for a while, impressed, in spite of themselves, by the vivid presentment of Gourlay's manhood on the day that had scared them all. The baker felt inclined to cry out on his cruelty for keeping his wife suffering to gratify his wrath; but the sudden picture of the man's courage changed that feeling to another of admiring awe: a man so defiant of the angry heavens might do anything. And so with the others; they hated Gourlay, but his bravery was a fact of nature which they could not disregard; they knew themselves smaller, and said nothing for a while. Tam Brodie, the most brutal among them, was the first to recover. Even he did not try to belittle at once, but he felt the subtle discomfort of the situation, and relieved it by bringing the conversation back to its usual channel.

'That was at the boy's birth, Mr Coe?' said he.

'Ou ay, just the laddie. It was a' richt when the lassie came. It was Doctor Dandy brocht *her* hame, for Munn was deid by that time, and Dandy had his place.'

'What will Gourlay be going to make of him?' the Provost asked. 'A doctor or a minister or wha-at?'

'Deil a fear o' that,' said Brodie, 'he'll take him into the business! It's a' that he's fit for. He's an infernal dunce, just his father owre again, and the Dominie thrashes him remorseless! I hear my own weans speaking o't. Ou, it seems he's just a perfect numbskull!'

'Ye couldn't expect ainything else from a son of Gourlay,' said the Provost.

Conversation languished. Some fillip was needed to bring it to an easy flow, and the simultaneous scrape of their feet turning round showed the direction of their thoughts.

'A dram would be very acceptable now,' murmured Sandy Toddle, rubbing his chin.

'Ou, we wouldna be the waur o't,' said Tam Wylie.

'We would be all the better of a little drope,' smirked the Deacon.

And they made for the Red Lion for the matutinal dram.

7

Embro To The Ploy

ROBERT GARIOCH

In simmer, whan aa sorts foregether
in Embro to the ploy,
fowk seek out friens to hae a blether,
or faes they'd fain annoy;
smorit wi British Railways' reek
frae Glesca or Glen Roy
or Wick, they come to hae a week
of cultivatit joy,
       or three,
in Embro to the ploy.

Americans wi routh of dollars,
wha drink our whisky neat,
wi Sasunachs and Oxford Scholars
are eydent for the treat
of music sedulously high-tie
at thirty-bob a seat;
Wop opera performed in Eytie
to them's richt up their street,
       they say,
in Embro to the ploy.

Furthgangan Embro folk come hame
for three weeks in the year,
and find Auld Reekie no the same,
fu sturrit in a steir.
The stane-faced biggins whaur they froze
and suppit puirshous leir
of cultural cauld-kale and brose
see cantraips unco queer
                              thae days
in Embro to the ploy.

The tartan tred wad gar ye lauch;
nae problem is owre teuch.
Your surname needna end in -*och;*
they'll cleik ye up the cleuch.
A puckle dollar bills will aye
preive Hiram Teufelsdrockh,
a septary of Clan McKay,
it's maybe richt eneuch,
                              verfluch!
in Embro to the ploy.

The auld High Schule, whaur monie a skelp
of triple-tonguit tawse
has gien a hyst-up and a help
towards Doctorates of Laws,
nou hears, for Ramsay's cantie rhyme,
loud pawmies of applause
frae folk that pey a pund a time
to sit on wudden raws
                              gey hard
in Embro to the ploy.

The haly kirk's Assembly-haa
nou fairly coups the creel
wi Lindsay's Three Estaitis, braw
devices of the Deil.
About our heids the satire stots
like hailstanes till we reel;
the bawrs are in auld-farrant Scots,
it's maybe jist as weill,
                              imphm,
in Embro to the ploy.

The Epworth Haa wi wunner did
behold a pipers' bicker;
wi *hadarid* and *hindarid*
the air gat thick and thicker.
Cumha na Cloinne pleyed on strings
torments a piper quicker
to get his dander up, by jings,
than thirty u.p. liquor,
                              hooch aye!
in Embro to the ploy.

The Northern British Embro Whigs
that stayed in Charlotte Square,
they fairly wad hae tined their wigs
to see the Stuarts there,
the bleidan Earl of Moray and aa
weill-pentit and gey bare;
Our Queen and Princess, buskit braw,
enjoyed the hale affair
                              (see Press)
in Embro to the ploy.

Whan day's anomalies are cled
in decent shades of nicht,
the Castle is transmogrified
by braw electric licht.
The toure that bields the Bruce's croun
presents an unco sicht
mair sib to Wardour Street nor Scone,
wae's me for Scotland's micht,
                              says I
in Embro to the ploy.

A happening, incident, or splore
affrontit them that saw
a thing they'd never seen afore—
in the McEwan Haa:
a lassie in a wheelie-chair
wi naething on at aa,
jist like my luck! I wasna there,
it's no the thing ava,
                              tut-tut,
in Embro to the ploy.

The Café Royal and Abbotsford
are filled wi orra folk
whaes stock-in-trade's the scrievit word,
or twicet-scrievit joke.
Brains, weak or strang, in heavy beer,
or ordinary, soak.
Quo yin: This yill is aafie dear,
I hae nae clinks in poke,
                              nor fauldan-money,
in Embro to the ploy.

The auld Assemby-rooms, whaur Scott
foregethert wi his fiers,
nou see a gey kenspeckle lot
ablow the chandeliers.
Til Embro drouths the Festival Club
a richt godsend appears;
it's something new to find a pub
that gaes on sairvan beers
                              eftir hours
in Embro to the ploy.

Jist pitten-out, the drucken mobs
frae howffs in Potterraw,
fleean, to hob-nob wi the Nobs,
ran to this Music Haa,
Register Rachel, Cougait Kate,
Nae-neb Nellie and aa
stauchert about amang the Great,
what fun! I never saw
                              the like,
in Embro to the ploy.

They toddle hame doun lit-up streets
filled wi synthetic joy;
aweill, the year brings few sic treats
and muckle to annoy.
There's monie hartsom braw high-jinks
mixed up in this alloy
in simmer, whan aa sorts foregether
in Embro to the ploy.

POLSKA

Mrs Coolie-Hoo's Pole

FRED URQUHART

The three women-porters were having a fly cup in the Porters'
Room before the Edinburgh-Aberdeen train came in at four
o'clock. 'Have another sandwich, ladies,' Mrs Lumsden said.
'We might as well eat them up.'

'Oh, but we shouldnie,' Mrs Mutch said, helping herself to
one and biting it almost in halves. 'It's no' fair to eat a' yer Spam.
Lookit the points ye have to gi'e for it!'

'Ach, the hetter awa' the sooner peace!' Mrs Lumsden laughed.
'We'll ha'e mair points next month!'

'Save some room for thae cakes I bought,' Nancy Young said.
'I had to stand for half an 'oor in a queue at McBride's to get
them. I wonder if it was worth it!'

'They look awfie nice,' Mrs Lumsden said. 'McBride's ha'e
the best cakes in the toon.'

'But when ye think o' the lovely things ye used to get afore
the war!' Mrs Mutch said. 'Things wi' whipped cream and
marzipan . . . Ummm, it makes ma teeth water just to think
aboot them!'

Although she was always the slowest at any jobs they had to
do, Mrs Mutch was the quickest eater. 'I've had a lot mair
experience than you twa,' she said often to the two younger
women. 'That's what comes o' havin' a large family and aye
havin' a race for the tastiest bites!'

'Umm, they're no' bad for wartime,' she said after she had sampled the first cake. 'They're delicious!'

'Leave that yin for me,' Mrs Lumsden said, pointing a skinny black-nailed finger at it.

'Another cake, Mrs Mutch?'

'No, I couldnie. I'm up to the beads!' Mrs Mutch put her hands on her stomach and belched. 'Excuse me!'

'Ye're quite excusable!' Nancy said, giggling.

'There's Mrs Coolie-Hoo!' Mrs Lumsden cried, glancing out of the window. 'It's time we were awa'.' She stood up and began to shove the cups and empty paper bags back into a small cardboard suitcase. 'We still have that van at Number Three to empty afore the four o'clock comes in. If we dinnie hurry up we'll ha'e auld Pin-Leg on oor track.'

' "Get a move on there! What the so-and-so dae ye think ye're dawdlin' at? You weemen are a' alike." ' Nancy Young giggled as she imitated old Pin-Leg's querulous voice. ' "If I had baith o' ma legs I'd be worth a dozen o' ye." '

'He's an auld nark,' Mrs Mutch said. 'Still, he's no' bad sometimes. Come on!'

Mrs Coolie-Hoo was arranging the cups on her tea-trolley when they passed. She was a small thin woman with a gentle face, genteelly dressed but wearing a small woollen cap that sat strangely on her straggly grey hair. It was her habit of wearing these little caps, pink and red and orange, that had made the porters give her her nick-name. She nodded and said 'Good afternoon,' but she made no move to open a conversation when they said: 'It's right cauld, isn't it?' They passed on to Platform Three where a large luggage van was waiting to be emptied.

'She's a funny soul that,' Mrs Lumsden said. 'D'ye ken for all the time she's been at the station I've never said onythin' to her beyond a guid day or a bad yin. She's real funny.'

'So would you be, too, if ye had a man like hers,' Nancy said.

They stopped. 'Oho! Have ye been hearin' somethin'?' said Mrs Mutch.

'I didnie know ye kent her,' said Mrs Lumsden.

'I dinnie,' Nancy said. 'But I was hearin' things.'

'Ay?' Mrs Mutch said. 'What kind o' things?'

But Nancy did not answer. They had reached the barrier of Number Three platform and they saw old Pin-Leg looking anxiously for them. He waved them on, and shouted something, and they broke into a run. Mrs Mutch, shambling behind the other two in her patched shoes, pushed up her porter's cap which was always falling forward over her eyes, and said to herself that Nancy was a bitch not to have told them sooner. She might have tellt us at tea-time, she said to herself. She kens fine that we're all dying to ken about Mrs Coolie-Hoo.

Nancy knew this, so she took her time about it. She reached the van before the others and scrambled in and climbed over the luggage to the back. 'I'll chuck the stuff oot,' she cried. 'Here, catch!'

'I'll chuck you!' Mrs Lumsden cried. 'And it'll no' be under the chin!'

'No, we'll leave that to Charlie,' Nancy shouted, winking at old Pin-Leg.

He grunted something under his breath. Mrs Mutch, who was the only one who overheard, laughed. 'Ye're a lad, Charlie!' she said, giving him a dig with her fat elbow.

'Less o' yer imperince,' he said, 'And get a haud o' that trolley. D'ye think ye came here to make jokes? You weemen!'

Mrs Mutch wrestled the trolley into position, then she stood pushing back her cap while waiting for Nancy and Mrs Lumsden to throw out the stuff.

'Here's the morn's dinner!' Nancy cried, pitching out a pair of rabbits. They struck Mrs Mutch on the chest and she cried: 'Here, here, Nancy Young! I'm wantin' a fur all right, but it's a Silver Fox I want! None o' yer cheap rabbit-skin dirt!'

'Here's some mair!' Nancy cried. She came to the door of the van, holding them up. 'Oh, the wee wee ones! Fancy killing them. What a shame, isn't it, Charlie?'

'Get on wi' yer work and dinnie blether so much,' Charlie grumbled. 'You weemen! Yer heads are just fu' o' a lot o' dirt.'

'Now, that'll dae ye, Charlie,' Mrs Lumsden said. 'We're for none o' yer auld-fashioned jaw. I'll have ye know that I went through ma hair wi' a small-tooth comb no later than last night!'

'Then ye must ha'e combed a' yer brains oot along wi' the other dirt,' the old man said. 'Look where ye're puttin' that case! That doesnie go on that barra.'

Mrs Mutch's trolley was almost full. 'Here, here Nancy, that's enough!' she cried. 'I'm no' a horse!'

'No, but ye're a cuddy,' Charlie said. 'And a gey stupid yin at that!'

'Less o' yer lip,' Mrs Mutch said. She leaned her elbows on the end of the trolley and said: 'Noo, Nancy, what was this ye were goin' to tell us aboot Mrs Coolie-Hoo?'

'Well now,' Nancy said, leaning against the door of the van. 'Last night I was speakin' to Bunty Robison and she tellt me . . .'

'Ye can easy tell yer story and carry on wi' yer work at the same time,' old Pin-Leg said. 'You weemen! I never saw onythin' like it. Yer tongues would just clish-clash a' day long if ye got the chance and if there wasnie a man like me to see that ye got on wi' the job.'

'And what a man!' Mrs Lumsden said.

Nancy made a face at Charlie and said: 'Well, Bunty tellt me that Mrs Coolie-Hoo's name was Mrs Barclay Matheson and that her man's a doctor. He's an awfie drouth and they dinnie get on thegither. This Y.M.C.A. tea-trolley's her War Work.'

'Ach, I thought ye had somethin' to tell us about her,' Mrs Lumsden said, turning away and picking up a flat wooden box.

'Well, so I have,' Nancy said. 'I've tellt ye her real name, haven't I? Ye didnie ken afore that it was Barclay Matheson.'

'Ach, that doesnie matter much,' Mrs Lumsden said. 'She's been Mrs Coolie-Hoo since the first day she came to the station and she'll go on bein' Mrs Coolie-Hoo as far as I'm concerned.'

'And I tellt ye her man drank, didn't I?'

'Ach, lots o' men dae that,' Mrs Lumsden said. 'Lookit mine afore he ga'ed awa' to the war. Drunk every Saturday night as regular as clock-work and I didnie think a thing aboot it. I would ha'e thocht he was sickenin' for somethin' if he hadnie come hame weel-oiled.'

'But listen, I havenie tellt ye everythin' yet,' Nancy said. 'However, if ye dinnie want to hear it . . .'

'Go on, Nancy,' said Mrs Mutch. 'Never let on ye hear her!'

Nancy put down the case she had picked up and she looked about to see that Charlie wasn't within hearing. 'She's got a Pole!' she said in a stage-whisper.

Mrs Lumsden sat down on a pile of boxes. Mrs Mutch gave her head such a jerk that her cap fell forward over her eyes again.

'Her! Got a Pole!'

Nancy nodded.

'Ay, she's got a Pole. And what's more he's a young Pole. An officer.'

'Well, I never!' Mrs Lumsden said. 'This beats a'.'

'What's an auld hen like her doin' wi' a Pole?' she said after a while. 'He'll be nae guid to her.'

'Bunty Robison tellt me that her cousin that's the maid at Mrs Coolie-Hoo's tellt her that Mrs B. M. as she calls her was fair gone on him. She's auld enough to be his mither, too. He's there every night, sittin' back and drinkin' and smokin' fags, wi' auld Coolie-Hoo runnin' roond in circles, doin' things for him.'

'I help ma God!' Mrs Lumsden said. 'It's no' decent.'

'There was a Pole spoke to me in a bus once,' Mrs Mutch said.

'Was there?' The other two leaned forward enquiringly.

'Ay,' Mrs Mutch sighed. 'It was awfie crowded and he sat doon aside me. I was fair tremblin'. And then when he leaned forrit and spoke I could hardly answer; I was that flabbergasted.'

'What did he say?' Nancy said eagerly.

'He asked me if I'd tell him when we came to the Crossgate.' Mrs Mutch heaved a case on to the trolley, sighing with the effort and the remembrance. 'I mind I spoke aboot the weather and the war, but he didnie seem to speak much English. He just said Yes and No. But he thanked me awfie nicely when he rose to go oot. Clicked his heels and saluted and a'. I felt like a Duchess!'

She sighed again and prepared to wheel away the loaded trolley. 'He was terrible nice-lookin',' she said over her shoulder. 'Just like Gary Cooper, only better.'

'There's the four o'clock comin' in!' Pin-Leg shouted. 'Hurry up, ye'll just need to leave the emptyin' o' this van till after. But the morn's night you weemen had better no' put off so much time takin' yer tea or I'll be complainin' to those Higher Up.'

Again Nancy was first in the race along the platform. As she ran, clitter-clattering with her high heels, she reset her porter's cap at a jaunty angle and brushed the dust off her blue dungarees. She looked into the distance, looking for any good-looking officer who might be getting out of the train. She saw one and dashed past two or three different passengers who were looking for porters.

'Carry yer bag, sir?'

'Oh—er—' The young officer blushed. 'Dash it all, I say, but —er—I'm perfectly capable of carrying it myself.'

But Nancy grabbed it from him and made towards the barrier before he could grab it back.

Mrs Mutch was last again. She held both hands on her enormous bust, smoothing down her print overall, panting with exertion.

As she pushed back her porter's cap she saw that a crowd of soldiers were milling around Mrs Coolie-Hoo's trolley and that Mrs Coolie-Hoo was looking harassed. Thank God, I'm no' the only yin that gets trauchled, she said to herself.

She saw an old woman struggling with a case in a carriage-doorway and she tried to put on a sprint, but before she could get past the old woman shouted to her. Mrs Mutch sighed and stopped unwillingly. I dinnie see why I should aye be landed wi' the auld yins, she thought angrily. I wonder if this auld bee kens if her journey's really necessary?

When Nancy Young came back along the platform, having seen her officer into a taxi and having made him blush again when he gave her a shilling, she saw Mrs Coolie-Hoo trailing along beside the train with a cup of tea in each hand. She looked aimless and out of place on the busy platform, with people dashing past her. Evidently she had lost sight of whoever she was taking the tea to and she was craning her thin neck, looking for them.

'Here, ma! In here, ma!'

A cockney in battledress was hanging out of a window, signalling to her. The guard was waving his flag. Mrs Coolie-Hoo gave a little jump and began to run, slopping over the tea in her haste. She managed to shove the two half-empty cups into the soldier's hand as the train was on the move. He gave them to somebody behind him and leaned out, holding a coin.

'Here, ma!' he cried. 'Keep the change. Buy yourself something nice!'

Mrs Coolie-Hoo stood and looked foolishly at the coin. She made a vague gesture and ran a few steps, but the train was gathering speed. She shouted something, but the soldier grinned and waved and then withdrew into the carriage. Mrs Coolie-Hoo shrugged and sighed. And she gaped blankly at the coin again.

Nancy Young twisted her lips, annoyed at the old woman's ineffectiveness. Nancy would never have looked so bewildered if anybody had tipped her. She knew exactly the right attitude to take up.

She yawned and was thinking about going back to Platform Three to go on with the unloading of the van when she saw a Polish officer coming along the platform through the thinning crowd of passengers. He saluted Mrs Coolie-Hoo, clicking his heels and half-bowing. Mrs Mutch who had come up beside Nancy gave her a nudge and said: 'That must be the boy-friend!'

They went into the Third Class Waiting Room and watched out of the window. They saw Mrs Coolie-Hoo hold out her hand, pointing to the coin and then to the disappearing train. She was laughing as if at a great joke. The Pole nodded and smiled. Then when Mrs Coolie-Hoo said something he frowned, but after a moment's hesitation he took the coin and put it in his trousers'-pocket. 'She's got it bad,' Nancy whispered. 'All the same he *is* a good-looker.'

During the next few weeks the Pole came a lot to the station. The three women-porters looked for his visits as eagerly as Mrs Coolie-Hoo seemed to do herself. Almost every day Nancy had some new tit-bit to tell which she had got from Bunty Robison. And what gossip Bunty and her cousin were not able to supply Nancy made up for herself.

Mrs Coolie-Hoo usually left the station in the evenings about the same time as the three women; just after the six-thirty train. One night the Pole was waiting for her at the entrance. The three women nodded and said 'Good evening' to him as they passed out into the blackout. They took it in turns to look round every two or three yards to see Mrs Coolie-Hoo and him following. 'He's takin' her arm noo,' Mrs Mutch whispered. 'He'll be takin' her to the pictures very likely,' Nancy said. 'Ay, they'll be goin' to see *The Woman Always Pays*!' Mrs Lumsden said. 'Och, maybe it's his turn to pay the night,' Mrs Mutch said. 'Never on yer Nellie Duff!' Nancy giggled. 'He doesnie look the kind.'

The three women stopped to wait for their bus at a stop beside a Gentlemen's Lavatory. Mrs Coolie-Hoo and her escort passed them, and Mrs Coolie-Hoo said 'Good evening.' They walked a few yards and then stood on the other side of the bus-stop. 'They dinnie believe in waitin' in queues surely!' Nancy whispered.

The women talked a lot, but none of them was really interested in what they were saying. They kept glancing along at the couple, straining their ears to overhear what was being said and repeating it in whispers under their own conversation.

Suddenly Mrs Mutch gave Nancy a tremendous dig and whispered: 'Watch this!'

The Pole was shuffling about, and at first the women thought he was dancing. But he began to hover from one leg to another, jumping up and down in an exaggerated way like a little boy. The women were so fascinated that they forgot to keep up their camouflaged conversation.

'Please, mummy, please!' the Pole cried. 'Please, I want to go upstairs!'

'Well, darling, run along!' said Mrs Coolie-Hoo, giggling. 'You'll have to hurry up, the bus'll soon be here.'

When the bus came the three women got in and went to the front. They sat in silence and never once did they look round to where Mrs Coolie-Hoo and the Pole were sitting. And it was only after they had got off that Nancy Young put into words what they had all been feeling. 'Mummy!' she said. 'Mummy by the livin' God!'

9

The Football Match

GEORGE BLAKE

The surge of the stream was already apparent in the Dumbarton
Road. Even though only a few wore favours of the Rangers blue,
there was that of purpose in the air of hurrying groups of men
which infallibly indicated their intention. It was almost as if they
had put on uniform for the occasion, for most were attired as
Danny was in decent dark suits under rainproofs or overcoats,
with great flat caps of light tweed on their heads. Most of them
smoked cigarettes that shivered in the corners of their mouths as
they fiercely debated the prospects of the day. Hardly one of
them but had his hands deep in his pockets.

The scattered procession, as it were of an order almost religious,
poured itself through the mean entrance to the subway station at
Partick Cross. The decrepit turnstiles clattered endlessly, and there
was much rough good-humoured jostling as the devotees
bounded down the wooden stairs to struggle for advantageous
positions on the crowded platform. Glasgow's subway system is
of high antiquarian interest and smells very strangely of age. Its
endless cables, whirling innocently over the pulleys, are at once
absurd and fascinating, its signalling system a matter for the
laughter of a later generation. But to Danny and the hundreds
milling about him there was no strange spectacle here: only a
means of approach to a shrine; and strongly they pushed and

wrestled when at length a short train of toy-like dimensions rattled out of the tunnel into the station.

It seemed full to suffocation already, but Danny, being alone and ruthless in his use of elbow and shoulder, contrived somehow to squeeze through a narrow doorway on to a crowded platform. Others pressed in behind him while official whistles skirled hopelessly without, and before the urgent crowd was forced back at last and the door laboriously closed, he was packed right among taller men of his kind, his arms pinned to his sides, his lungs so compressed that he gasped.

'For the love o' Mike . . .' he pleaded.

'Have ye no' heard there's a fitba' match the day, wee man?' asked a tall humorist beside him.

Everybody laughed at that. For them there was nothing odd or notably objectionable in their dangerous discomfort. It was, at the worst, a purgatorial episode on the passage to Elysium. So they passed under the river, to be emptied in their hundreds among the red sandstone tenements of the South Side. Under the high banks of the Park a score of streams met and mingled, the streams that had come by train or tram or motor car or on foot to see the game of games.

Danny ran for it as soon as his feet were on earth's surface again, selecting in an experienced glance the turnstile with the shortest queue before it, ignoring quite the mournful column that waited without hope at the Unemployed Gate. His belly pushed the bar precisely as his shilling smacked on the iron counter. A moment later he was tearing as if for dear life up the long flight of cindered steps leading to the top of the embankment.

He achieved his favourite position without difficulty: high on one of the topmost terraces and behind the eastern goal. Already the huge amphitheatre seemed well filled. Except where the monstrous stands broke the skyline there were cliffs of human faces, for all the world like banks of gravel, with thin clouds of tobacco smoke drifting across them. But Danny knew that thousands were still to come to pack the terraces to the point of suffocation, and, with no eyes for the sombre strangeness of the spectacle, he proceeded to establish himself by setting his arms firmly along the iron bar before him and making friendly, or at least argumentative, contact with his neighbours.

He was among enthusiasts of his own persuasion. In consonance with ancient custom the police had shepherded supporters of the

8

Rangers to one end of the ground and supporters of the Celtic to the other—so far as segregation was possible with such a great mob of human beings. For the game between Glasgow's two leading teams had more in it than the simple test of relative skill. Their colours, blue and green, were symbolic. Behind the rivalry of players, behind even the commercial rivalry of limited companies, was the dark significance of sectarian and racial passions. Blue for the Protestants of Scotland and Ulster, green for the Roman Catholics of the Free State; and it was a bitter war that was to be waged on that strip of white-barred turf. All the social problems of a hybrid city were to be sublimated in the imminent clash of mercenaries.

The Celtic came first, strangely attractive in their white and green, and there was a roar from the western end of the ground. ('Hefty-looking lot o' bastards,' admitted the small, old man at Danny's side.) They were followed by a party of young men in light-blue jerseys; and then it seemed that the low-hanging clouds must split at the impact of the yell that rose to greet them from forty thousand throats. The referee appeared, jaunty in his shorts and khaki jacket; the linesmen, similarly attired, ran to their positions. In a strange hush, broken only by the thud of footballs kicked by the teams uneasily practising, the captains tossed for ends. Ah! Rangers had won and would play with the sou'-westerly wind, straight towards the goal behind which Danny stood in his eagerness. This was enough to send a man off his head. Good old Rangers—and to hell with the Pope! Danny gripped the iron bar before him. The players trotted limberly to their positions. For a moment there was dead silence over Ibrox Park. Then the whistle blew, a thin, curt, almost feeble announcement of glory.

For nearly two hours thereafter Danny Shields lived far beyond himself in a whirling world of passion. All sorts of racial emotions were released by this clash of athletic young men; the old clans of Scotland lived again their ancient hatreds in this struggle for goals. Not a man on the terraces paused to reflect that it was a spectacle cunningly arranged to draw their shillings, or to remember that the twenty-two players were so many slaves of a commercial system, liable to be bought and sold like fallen women, without any regard for their feelings as men. Rangers had drawn their warriors from all corners of Scotland—lads from mining villages, boys from Ayrshire farms and even an undergraduate from the

University of Glasgow. Celtic likewise had ranged the industrial belt and even crossed to Ulster and the Free State for men fit to win matches so that dividends might accrue. But for such as Danny they remained peerless and fearless warriors, saints of the Blue or the Green as it might be; and in delight in the cunning moves of them, in their tricks and asperities, the men on the terraces found release from the drabness of their own industrial degradation.

That release they expressed in ways extremely violent. They exhorted their favourites to dreadful enterprises of assault and battery. They loudly questioned every decision of the referee. In moments of high tension they raved obscenely, using a language ugly and violent in its wealth of explosive consonants.

Yet that passionate horde has its wild and liberating humours. Now and again a flash of rough jocularity would release a gust of laughter, so hearty that it was as if they rejoiced to escape from the bondage of their own intensity of partisanship. Once in a while a clever movement by one of the opposition team would evoke a mutter of unwilling but sincere admiration. They were abundantly capable of calling upon their favourites to use their brawn, but they were punctilious in the observation of the unwritten laws that are called those of sportsmanship. They constituted, in fact, a stern but ultimately reliable jury, demanding of their entertainers the very best they could give, insisting that the spectacle be staged with all the vigour that could be brought to it.

The Old Firm—thus the evening papers conventionally described the meeting of Rangers and Celtic. It was a game fought hard and fearless and merciless, and it was the rub of the business that the wearers of the Blue scored seven minutes from half-time.

The goal was the outcome of a movement so swift that even a critic of Danny's perspicacity could hardly tell just how it happened. What is it to say that a back cleared from near the Rangers' goal; that the ball went on the wind to the nimble feet of Alan Morton on the left wing; that that small but intense performer carried it at lightning speed down the line past this man in green and white and then that; that he crossed before the menace of a charging back, the ball soaring in a lovely curve to the waiting centre; and that it went then like a rocket into a corner of the Celtic net, the goalkeeper sprawling in a futile endeavour to stop it? It was a movement completed almost as soon as it was begun, and Danny did not really understand it until he read his evening paper on the way home. But it was a goal, a goal for Rangers, and he went mad for a space.

With those about him he screamed his triumph, waving his cap wildly about his head, taunting most foully those who might be in favour of a team so thoroughly humiliated as the Celtic.

'Good old Alan!' screeched the young man behind. 'Ye've got the suckers bitched!'

'A piece of perfect bloody positioning,' gravely observed the scientist on Danny's left.

'Positioning, ma foot!' snorted Danny. 'It was just bloomin' good fitba! Will ye have a snifter, old fella?'

So they shared the half-mutchkin of raw whisky, the small man politely wiping the neck of the bottle with his sleeve before handing it back to Danny.

'That's a good dram, son,' he observed judicially.

Half-time permitted of discussion that was now, however, without its heat, the young man behind exploiting a critical theory of half-back play that kept some thirty men about him in violent controversy until the whistle blew again. Then the fever came back on them with redoubled fury. One-nothing for Rangers at half-time made an almost agonizing situation; and as the Celtic battled to equalize, breaking themselves again and again on a defence grimly determined to hold its advantage, the waves of green hurling themselves on rocks of blue, there was frenzy on the terraces.

When, five minutes before time, the men from the East were awarded a penalty kick, Danny's heart stopped beating for a space, and when the fouled forward sent the ball flying foolishly over the net, it nearly burst. The Rangers would win. 'Stick it, lads!' he yelled again and again. 'Kick the tripes out the dirty Papists!' The Rangers would win. They must win. . . . A spirt of whistle; and, by God, they had won!

In immediate swift reaction, Danny turned then and, without a word to his neighbours, started to fight his way to the top of the terracing and along the fence that crowned it to the stairs and the open gate. To the feelings of those he jostled and pushed he gave not the slightest thought. Now the battle was for a place in the Subway, and he ran as soon as he could, hurtling down the road, into the odorous maw of Copland Road station and through the closing door of a train that had already started on its journey northwards.

10

The Fell Sergeant

NEIL MUNRO

It is ill enough to have to die in Glenaora at any season, but to get the word for travelling from it on yon trip in the spring of the year is hard indeed. The gug-gug will halloo in your ears to bid you bide a wee and see the red of the heather creep on Tom-an-dearc; the soft and sap-scented winds will come in at the open door, and you will mind, maybe, of a day long-off and lost when you pulled the copper leaves of the bursting oak and tossed them among a girl's hair. Oh! the long days and the strong days! They will come back to you like the curious bit in a tune that is vexatious and sweet, and not for words or a set thought. You will think of the lambs on the slopes, of the birds tearing through the thousand ways in the woods, of the magic hollows in below the thick-sown pines, of the burns, deep at the bottom of *eas* and corri, spilling like gold on a stair. And then, it may be, Solomon Carrier's cart goes by to the town, the first time since the drifts went off the high road; you hear the clatter of the iron shoes, and your mind will go with him to the throng street where the folks are so kind and so free.

But to turn back for the last at that time on Lecknamban must come sorest of all. For Lecknamban has seven sheilings hidden in its hills, where the grass is long and juicy, and five burns that are aye on the giggle like girls at a wedding, and the Aora daunders down in front of the knowe, full of fish for the Duke alone, but bonny for earl or caird.

It was in this same glen, in this same Lecknamban, in the spring of a year, a woman was at her end. She was a woman up in years but not old, a black Bana-Mhuileach who had seen pleasant things and trials like all who come to this queer market-place; but now when the time was come to take the long road with no convoy, only the good times were in her recollection. And though Glenaora was not her calf-country (for she came but a year ago to bide with a friend), she was sweir to turn heel on a place so cosy.

She sat propped up in a box-bed, on pillows, with her face to the open door, and the friendly airs of the countryside came in to stir her hair. With them came scents of the red earth and the grass, birch-tree, and myrtle, from the moor. But more than all they brought her who was at her end a keen craving for one more summer of the grand world. Strong in her make and dour at the giving-in, she kept talking of the world's affairs and foolishness to the folk about her, who were waiting the Almighty's will and the coming of the stretching-board. Her fingers picked without a stop at the woolly bits of the blankets, and her eyes were on as much of the knowe below the house as she could see out at the open door. It was yellow at the foot with flowers, and here and there was a spot of blue from the cuckoo-brogue.

'Women, women,' she said with short breaths, 'I'm thinking aye, when I see the flowers, of a man that came from these parts to Duart. He sang "Mo Nighean Dubh" in a style was never heard before in our place, and he once brought me the scented cuckoo-brogues from Aora.' Said the goodwife, 'Aoirig, poor woman, it is not the hour for ancient old *sgeuls*; be thinking of a canny going.'

'Going! it was aye going with me,' said the woman in the bed. 'And it was aye going when things were at their best and I was the keener for them.' 'It's the way of God, my dear, ochanie!' said one of the two Tullich sisters, putting a little salt in a plate for the coming business.

'O God! it's the hard way, indeed. And I'm not so old as you by two or three clippings.' 'Peace, Aoirig, heart; you had your own merry times, and that's as much as most of us have claim to.'

'Merry times! merry times!' said Aoirig, humped among the bedding, her mind wandering.

Curls of the peat-reek coiled from the floor among the *cabars* or through the hole in the roof; a lamb ran by the door bleating for its mother, and the whistling of an *uiseag* high over the grass where his nest lay ran out to a thin thread of song. The sound of it troubled the dying woman, and she asked her friends to shut the door. The goodwife was throng among chests and presses looking for sheets, shrouds, and dead-caps.

'It's a pity,' said she, 'you brought no grave-clothes with you from Mull, my dear.' 'Are you grudging me yours?' asked Aoirig, coming round from wandering.

'No, not grudging; fine ye ken it, cousin. But I know ye have them, and it's a pity you should be dressed in another's spinning than your own.' 'Ay, they're yonder sure enough: clean and ready. And there's more than that beside them. The linen I should have brought to a man's home.'

'You and your man's home! Is it Duart, my dear, among your own folk, or down to Inishail you would have us take you?' 'Duart is homely and Inishail is holy, sure enough, but I would have it Kilmalieu. They tell me it's a fine kirkyard; but I never had the luck to see it.'

'It's well enough, I'll not deny, and it would not be so far to take you. Our folk have a space of their own among the Mac-Vicars, below the parson.'

The woman in the bed signed for a sip of water, and they had it fast at her lips.

'Could you be putting me near the Macnicols?' she asked in a weakening voice. 'The one I speak of was a Macnicol.'

'Ay, ay,' said the goodwife; 'they were aye gallant among the girls.' 'Gallant he was,' said the one among the blankets. 'I see him now. The best man I ever saw. It was at a wedding—'

Maisie was heating a death-shift at the peat-fire, turning it over in her hands, letting the dry airs into every seam and corner. Looking at her preparation, the dying woman caught back her breath to ask why such trouble with a death-shift.

'Ye would not have it on damp and cold,' said Maisie, settling the business. 'I doubt it'll be long in the sleeves, woman, for the goodwife has a lengthy reach.'

'It was at a marriage in Glenurchy,' said Aoirig in a haver, the pillows slipping down behind her back. 'Yonder he is. A slim straight lad. Ronnal, O Ronnal, my hero! What a dancer! not his match in Mull. Aye so——'

A foot could be heard on the road, and one of the two sisters ran out, for she knew whom it would be. They had sent word to the town by Solomon in the morning for Macnicol the wright to come up with the stretching-board, thinking there was but an hour more for poor Aoirig.

Macnicol's were the footsteps, and there he was with the stretching-board under his arm—a good piece of larch rubbed smooth by sheet and shroud, and a little hollow worn at the head. He was a fat man, rolling a bit to one side on a short leg, gross and flabby at the jowl, and thick-lipped; but he might have been a swanky lad in his day, and there was a bit of good-humour in the corner of his eye, where you will never see it when one has been born with the uneasy mind. He was humming to himself as he came up the brae a Badenoch ditty they have in these parts on the winter nights, gossiping round the fire. Whom he was going to stretch he had no notion, except it was a woman and a stranger to the glen.

The sister took him round to the corner of the house, and in at the byre door, and told him to wait. 'It'll not be long now,' she said.

'Then she's still to the fore,' said the wright. 'I might have waited on the pay-master's dram at Three Bridges if I had ken't. Women are aye thrawn about dying. They'll put it off to the last, when a man would be glad to be taking the road. Who is she, poor woman?'

'A cousin-german of Nanny's,' said the sister, putting a bottle before him, and whipping out for some bannock and cheese. He sat down on a shearing-stool, facing the door half open between the byre he was in and the kitchen where Aoirig was at the dying. The stretching-board leaned against the wall outside.

'Aye so gentle, so kind,' the woman in the bed was saying in her last dover. 'He kissed me first on a day like this. And the blue flowers from Aora?'

In the byre the wright was preeing the drink and paying little heed to food. It was the good warm stuff they brew on the side of Lochow, the heart of the heart of the barley-fields, with the taste of gall and peat, and he mellowed with every quaich, and took to the soft lilting of Niall Ban's song:

> ' "I am the Sergeant fell but kind,
>   (Ho! ho! heroes, agus ho-e-ro!)
> I only lift but the deaf and blind,
>   The wearied-out and the rest-inclined.

Many a booty I drive before,
Through the glens, through the glens,"
said *the Sergeant Mor.'*

Ben the house the goodwife was saying the prayers for the dying woman the woman should have said for herself while she had wind for it, but Aoirig harped on her love-tale. She was going fast, and the sisters, putting their hands to her feet, could feel that they were cold as the rocks. Maisie's arms were round her, and she seemed to have the notion that here was the grip of death, for she pushed her back. 'I am not so old—so old. There is Seana, my neighbour at Duart—long past the four-score and still spinning —I am not so old—God of grace—so old—and the flowers—'

A grey shiver went over her face; her breast heaved and fell in; her voice stopped with a gluck in the throat.

The women stirred round fast in the kitchen. Out on the clay floor the two sisters pushed the table and laid a sheet on it, the goodwife put aside the pillows and let Aoirig's head fall back on the bed. Maisie put her hand to the clock and stopped it.

'Open the door, open the door!' cried the goodwife, turning round in a hurry and seeing the door still shut.

One of the sisters put a finger below the sneck and did as she was told, to let out the dead one's ghost.

Outside, taking the air, to get the stir of the strong waters out of his head, was the wright. He knew what the opening of the door meant, and he lifted his board and went in with it under his arm. A wafting of the spring smells came in at his back, and he stood with his bonnet in his hand. 'So this is the end o't?' he said in a soft way, stamping out the fire on the floor.

He had but said it when Aoirig sat up with a start in the bed, and the women cried out. She opened her eyes and looked at the man, with his fat face, his round back, and ill-made clothes, and the death-deal under his oxter, and then she fell back on the bed with her face stiffening.

'Here's the board for ye,' said the wright, his face spotted white and his eyes staring. 'I'll go out a bit and take a look about me. I once knew a woman who was terribly like you, and she came from Mull.'

11

The Long Walk

CLIFFORD HANLEY

Some years ago, everybody started talking about a daunting middle-aged lady, Dr Barbara Moore, who appeared to live on honey and her own conversation, and walked single-handed from John o' Groats to Land's End. This infuriated many people with legs, and several of them travelled to John o' Groats to show that they could do the same thing faster, or backwards, or pushing peas with their noses. For a while it looked as if long-distance walking might oust bigamy as a national sport. It didn't happen, of course, but it was touch and go at the time.

At first, the field was left open to athletes and specialized maniacs, but when Billy Butlin announced that he would give real cash money for the winner of a walking race the length of Britain, one realized that amazing scenes would be witnessed. Road, rail and air services to the north were jammed as the British public moved in for the easiest thousand pounds ever offered. There were nearly as many reporters and photographers as there were competitors, and the newspaper I worked for had the brilliant notion that I should not merely report the fun, but get right in among it, on my feet. It sounded fine, and precisely fitted my philosophy that Anybody Can Do Anything. I started reading *Scouting for Boys* and experimenting with thick socks and thin socks and socks full of talcum powder, and underwear made of knotted rope.

I was not underestimating the grimness of the task. Though fit and sinewy and well-shaped when I pulled in my paunch, I had been out of competitive sport for some little time. My usual form of invigorating exercise was a careful stroll across a hotel lounge and a quick tomato juice. I wasn't too sure about shoes and boots either, but I went into training at once, trying out my stock of footwear on alternative evenings and walking as much as two miles with my chest thrown out and my eye on the money. There was snow on the ground.

Sanity intervened, and for the sake of my professional commitments, I decided that I wouldn't go the whole distance and cheat some genuine enthusiast of the prize. I would walk only halfway, or partway, to get the atmosphere of the thing. In fact, I would walk from John o' Groats to Wick, which is all of nineteen miles. And then I would still be available to write a sizzling story of How It Felt. Nobody laughed at this. The kind of people I know do not sneer at a walk of nineteen miles.

I still think it's a pity Mr Butlin didn't stick in and make the mass walk an annual fest, because nobody in Caithness, or the newspaper business, has ever seen anything like it in history. The snow was still on the ground up there, and at Renfrew Airport numbers of frantic reporters were trying to bribe their way on to crowded planes to be there on time. In dead of winter, the hotels in far-off Wick were bulging with free-spending custom and the wee shops were praying for rapid delivery of gumboots and corn plasters and aspirin for the biggest bonanza of all time. Although the air was as cold as a scalpel, the streets were humming with people all glowing with hysteria. The natives were hysterical too—and not only from the sight of so much dough pouring in. Up in Wick, they *liked* us. The Caithness folk, whom I had never met before, fairly shine with simple kindness. With snow added, it felt like the Klondyke, but without the killing fever.

Every few minutes of the day and night, straggling prospectors were finding their way in. Scout halls and drill halls and church halls were opened as dormitories. A sad, shifty little woman turned up at my hotel to ask for a temporary job as a waitress in order to grubstake her entry for the Walk. She agreed that she wouldn't be a very fast waitress because she suffered horrible with her feet. A slim young man was observed trying out his legs in a morning suit with top hat and cane. The newspaper gang positively had the Klondyke feeling. Wick was a million miles from home, it was impossible *not* to get plenty of stories, and nobody at head-office could have any idea how much bribe-money it was costing. Hard-eyed blokes from *The People* or *The Mirror* were exchanging brotherly quips with gentlemen from *The Times* newspaper. Improbable, nubile young women, who must have been starlets looking for a break, were being plied with dry Martinis and interviewed in dark corners.

On the day of the Walk, Wick began to empty in a panic. It was still nineteen miles to the starting line, and the long narrow road was strung out with terror-stricken hitch-hikers and taxis and trucks. There isn't much at John o' Groats except a hotel and a few buildings and that multi-sided folly that John built. I never expect to see it again, because it wouldn't look the same without Billy Butlin's marquee and a mob of lunatics spilling everywhere. The sun shone in the middle of the day. John o' Groats is really the end of the line. Across the water to the north was the island of Stroma, brown-red in the sunlight and waiting for a buyer. I thought it might be nice to buy it, if I could move it somewhere else. A man from the *News of the World* offered me a slug from his pocket flask, and I recoiled in horror at the idea of competing half-sloshed, and took one.

There was a tubby little American, wearing pince-nez fastened to his hat by a chain, and a cellophane cover on his hat. He didn't believe in socks, and wore toeless sandals with polythene wrapped round his toes to keep them dry. He had a bundle of papers under his arm, and he was entering the walk to vindicate his disagreement with Einstein, whom he regarded as a good man but misguided.

'I have proved,' he told us, 'that e is not equal to mc squared, but to mc cubed.' Seven or eight reporters were crowded round him shouting questions into the wind and taking notes.

'What the hell is M C Q?' one of them asked me, because I was known to be a scientific fake.

'It's some kind of photographic developer,' I said happily. The other reporter wasn't walking nineteen miles that night, and therefore deserved no quarter. There was a woman in high-heeled shoes, with a brown coat and a pixie hood, and a string bag containing enough groceries to last for 500 miles. She walked about bent over to one side to balance the groceries. A girl was entering in a bathing costume. There were walkers in track suits and walkers in running shorts. Another woman was proposing to push a pram to the south of England. A syndicate had a trek cart loaded with their safari supplies. There were family parties spanning the generations. Somewhere down the road, Mr Butlin had an ambulance in wait to pick up collapsers. He knew what he was doing.

But in its crazy way it was magnificent. Three-quarters of the walkers had a slim hope of getting back to Wick on their feet, never mind Land's End. They were mad. They had no right to be getting in the way. But even if it's not true that Anybody Can Do Anything, it stuck out a mile that anybody could *try* anything. There were so many loons in for the race that it was hard to tell when it actually started. Humanity surged back and forth aimlessly till the news got through the crowd, and by that time the early birds were pounding down the road into the distance.

By then I had worked out the secret strategy. Since I wasn't going to finish the race, I didn't need to reserve my effort, and therefore, just for fun, I would be in the first rank of starters and run like hell all the way to Wick.

The honour of my newspaper, of my native city, of my family, was at stake. I and no other would be first past the Wick checkpoint, and *then* collapse.

What a pathetic fool I was. By the time I wormed my way through the tortoise group, the leader of the pack must have been two miles away, and these boys in front were no dilettantes. They meant to win, and they were the kind of tough-muscled swine who would tear off twenty miles to warm up for a sprint.

Still, it was possible to be in the first ten. Fifty? Hundred? Darkness started to come down almost at once. It was now clear why the clever lads had got off early. Inside half-an-hour, it was nearly impossible to jostle through the procession at the rear. And for the first time, the old competitive curse of humanity was beginning to show. The slow walkers had set themselves a timetable, and they were sticking to it to maintain their strength, but you could tell that they hated anybody who overtook them. The farther they walked, the more they hated the overtakers. The reality of those hundreds of miles must have been starting to loom at last. Most of them walked in groups, each forming a phalanx, so that to overtake you had to scramble into the packed snow at the roadside; and very soon, there was no polite giving way. We all had the lust for gold.

After three miles, walking alone, too quickly, in the dark,

on a road crowded with hostile strangers, I developed the conviction that the leaders must be away across the English border. I stuck to my plan of walking a hundred, running a hundred. It was all right, except for the occasional sight of other reporters swishing along in hired cars to look at us, and probably swigging from hip-flasks the while, and me not even in a position to justify any expenses till I got back to Wick.

One good thing happened. Halfway between John o' Groats and Wick there's a completely meaningless village called Keiss. I'm not trying to knock the place, it's only that I couldn't see any reason why it was there at all. Maybe it looks logical in summer, but at that time of year it baffled all conjecture. You might as well have put up an antique shop bang in the middle of Antarctica for all the sense it made. And it wasn't just a huddle of wee rustic cottages. It was a street of *tenements*. With street lamps. I looked it up yesterday in the atlas, and it's there all right. I had begun to wonder if the whole experience was a mirage caused by the Aurora Borealis. Anyway, what happened was that we all came shambling one by one out of the northern darkness into this main street and found the whole population of the district lined up on both sides to offer a rousing welcome to each and every fool. And this audience wasn't even walking or running, it was standing there, freezing to death and managing to radiate goodwill. I got stage fright. It's one thing staggering through a desert landscape and feeling gormless, but you know the feeling when you're up to something private and absurd and suddenly the stage-manager switches on the lights and there's a packed house out there all the time. I swerved off the road and tried to sneak down the pavement behind the crowd, hoping they would think I was an innocent householder who had nipped out to buy a tin of condensed milk. This was a total failure.

They could probably tell by the outfit that I wasn't a legitimate resident. I was togged up—and now I come to think of it, these little details of walkers' techniques should not be omitted—in what I have found by experiment to be the ideal set for physical heroism: checked sports jacket by Maxi Mann of Sauchiehall Street; Daks trousers; shirt, socks and cellular underwear by Marks and Spencer; string gloves by Copland and Lye; cotton showerproof by Swallow; tie by Munrospun; black leather, crepe-soled Flotillas by Clarks. I still have the shoes. Sometimes in thoughtful moments I take them out and kick them round the

living-room. I could have walked into any Mecca ballroom
without raising an eyebrow. Up in Keiss, I managed to get the
whole crowd on the west side of Main Street to turn their backs
on the road and pat me on the back as I slithered along the pavement. They had been keeping count, too. 'You're fine, lad,' they
shouted. 'There's only a hundred and eighteen in front of you.'

I suppose they cheered with as much enthusiasm for Number
800. These Caithness characters just don't wear out.

South of Keiss, it went all quiet and black and horrible again.
Let us draw a veil, for God's sake. About two miles short of Wick,
another of those reporter thugs drew alongside me in a black
Citroën, and I snarled quietly and tottered away till I realized he
was hanging out of the window and calling me by name. It was
my own photographer, a splendid Christian gentleman, who had
come out to persuade me to betray my trust by taking a lift, and
while I was wrestling with my conscience and dragging the car
door open, another hiker drew alongside and crumpled up
unconscious on the roadside. Oh boy, I loved that man. We
couldn't do anything else but lift him into the Citroën and rush
him to hospital, with me to hold his hand. It wasn't all that funny,
in fact. The unknown walker was as pale as snow, and for a
minute or two I thought he had died in my lap. But they took
him in cheerfully at the hospital and warmed him up and we
went down to the hotel in Wick.

The man from *The Times* newspaper had just wandered out
from the bar, drinking a large whisky, and he greeted me with a
gesture that nearly convinced me of English supremacy. He
rammed his own drink into my hand.

'Rather a newsy weekend,' he said affably, and I gulped and
said yes. Then I said, 'To what news are you referring to which?'
and I had one of those pricklings of the scalp that folk get in
tough detective stories.

'Princess Margaret's got engaged,' he said patiently. 'Hadn't
you heard?'

'God!' I said. 'She couldn't have waited another day!'

'It's handy for the Sundays,' he argued. There was no harm in
the man at all. He was taking a balanced view of the situation.
But who was going to want to read about heroic reporters
walking through endless Caithness nights when a whole princess
was available? With my life in ruins, I fell asleep over a dish
of stewed steak and went to bed. A lassie came and slipped five

or six hot water bottles in beside me and I went into a three-day coma. This was interrupted two hours later by Macnicol, a dangerous feature-writer from *The Express*, with the news that a hospital matron was throwing a late-night party, so I leapt from bed in a clatter of mangled bones and we whooped it up till three or four. We had to walk home too, and it rained.